"This book is a must read for any parent or guardian whose child is pursuing a career in show business. It is also a tremendous resource for any attorney, manager, or agent working in that area. Sally Gaglini delivers great wisdom, experience, and expertise."

—Andrew Velcoff, entertainment attorney, Atlanta

"Finally! Disguised as a book for parents of talented children, this is a must read for all of us working with young talent in the entertainment industry, including parents of stars in the making. It makes the law accessible to everyone with Fair Play, contracts, and state rules featured. Sally Gaglini's expertise and vast knowledge easily make this book the industry's definitive go-to guide for parents and employers of young performers."

—Anthony Resta, Paramount Studios, Los Angeles

"Gaglini's book demystifies the entertainment industry, helping emerging young artists (and their parents) make smart decisions as they pursue their dreams."

—Madeleine Steczynski, cofounder and executive director, ZUMIX, Boston

"Especially for parents of young talent, this is one tremendous read and resource. Sally Gaglini takes a no-nonsense approach and offers invaluable need-to-know information about working kids in the business. Her generous assessments about the entertainment industry, and her in-depth understanding of the law and what parents *and* employers need, are spot-on and transformative."

—Stanley Moger, president,
SFM Entertainment LLC, New York

"This book offers a wise, empathic, and masterful account of the opportunities and land mines of childhood stardom. Sally Gaglini has written *the guide.*"

—Zack Johnson, chief executive officer, Syndio, Chicago

"Sally Gaglini's book is an invaluable and enlightening parental guide for handling the emotional, educational, production, business, and legal pitfalls that can befall children who work in the entertainment industry."

—Stan Soocher, editor in chief, *Entertainment Law & Finance*; entertainment attorney; and associate professor, Music & Entertainment Industry Studies, University of Colorado Denver

# YOUNG
# PERFORMERS
# AT WORK

# YOUNG
## PERFORMERS
# AT WORK

## CHILD STAR
### SURVIVAL GUIDE

## SALLY R. GAGLINI

ZIP CELEBRITY MEDIA LLC

Published by Zip Celebrity Media LLC, Boston

Copyediting and Design: Girl Friday Productions
Cover Design: Paul Barrett

ISBN-13: 9780996368407
ISBN-10: 099636840X
e-ISBN: 9780996368414
Library of Congress Control Number: 2015909361

First Edition

Printed in the United States of America

*To Lou*

# CONTENTS

# PREFACE

There is one overriding principle that I wish to convey about *Young Performers at Work: Child Star Survival Guide*: empowering parents with essential information gives children their best hope for protection and success.

This book guides parents through typical challenges: safety and education, avoiding scams, staying with a child throughout a workday, baby casting, unions, reality shows, money and taxes, contracts and how kids may get out of them, and emancipation, along with other special considerations. The information is offered with a balanced perspective.

Over the years, I have represented young talent in certain matters and companies in others. My experience allows me to bring complicated issues into focus and deliberately tackle questions that both parents and companies have asked me behind closed doors. This book is a slice-of-life portrayal of what happens in the entertainment industry and why, using interviews with various industry professionals—an educator who specializes in teaching young performers, a model manager, children's model agents, a child labor specialist, and more. I've added some history of the entertainment industry to help better illustrate applicable laws and regulations and why talented working kids need both.

Since there are no specific federal laws protecting talented working child performers in the United States, keeping up with state laws can be daunting, even for lawyers and industry professionals. Consequently, state child performer laws are compiled and, in certain instances, discussed.

I think the time has come to acknowledge particular unsung heroes who unite the entertainment industry by giving their time, talent, passion, knowledge, and experience for the protection and support of young talent.

So take a seat. You are in for quite a ride.

# INTRODUCTION

In the beginning, I primarily worked during the day as a law clerk for the late Barry E. Rosenthal, an entertainment and corporate attorney. After work, I'd pretty much run through historic Faneuil Hall in Boston, Massachusetts, grab something cheap to eat, and attend classes at night at Suffolk University Law School. When I landed the job with Barry, I learned that much of my time with him would be spent working for his firm's client, the New Kids on the Block ("New Kids"). At the time, I wondered if the money spent for me to take music lessons at the Berklee School of Music (it wasn't a college yet) and the New England Conservatory in my teens would finally pay off.

During that really early period of my career, I made a startling discovery. Although the array of legal protections afforded to children involved in traditional family law disputes stacked up pretty nicely, when it came to guarding talented working kids from exploitation, protections were frustratingly harder to find—if they existed at all. In other words, some kids pretty much got the shaft. What an eye-opener!

In the aftermath of New Kids hitting the big time, the legal protection void in the entertainment industry for minors in Massachusetts was nearly impossible to miss. I remember Barry saying that it takes a performer three to five years to become an "overnight success," and the perception that the New Kids were instantaneously successful ignited a frenzy inside recording studios and on stages in Massachusetts to replicate that success. The music industry, a minefield even for adult performers, was especially challenging to navigate for young talent. The commercial landscape in almost every legal way imaginable proved to be less than ideal for young artists. Children were, in general, offered excessively long, one-sided contracts that were written completely in the company's favor. Parents and families were, more often than not, regrettably clueless.

Intending to make the process more fair to children and their families, I headed up to historic Beacon Hill as a pro bono advocate for children to introduce a bill that would enhance protections for child performers. The bill, An Act Relative to Entertainment Contracts for Children, was modeled in part on

New York's existing Arts and Cultural Affairs Law and established a systematic review of contracts and children's earnings by the state's probate court. The goal was to ensure a child a fair contract to sign by empowering a judge with discretion to appoint an independent guardian ad litem to review the contract, and to see to it that all or a portion of the child's earnings were preserved for him or her until he or she could claim the money at age eighteen. Mom and/or Dad (or another suitable person) would petition the court to serve as limited guardian(s) to watch over their child's earnings. In addition to helping children, the process would benefit the companies who contracted with children because, once the court approved the contract and its associated petitions, a child could not walk away from his or her contractual responsibilities. The company's investment, in other words, would be secure. With the support of dedicated legislators, their staffs, House counsel, the Children's Legislative Caucus, and then-governor William F. Weld, the bill became law in—a genuine rarity—one year.

Since graduating from law school, I have practiced a unique and satisfying blend of entertainment, advertising, probate, and family law. First hired as a staff attorney for Motorola, I eventually went into private practice. Rooted in my belief that it is important to give back professionally, my practice has included working on cases for families as a court-appointed and certified guardian ad litem for the state courts of Massachusetts on behalf of children, teens, and others who require special assistance. I also have taught entertainment law at my alma mater for many years. Finally, I continue to advocate for changes in the law to keep pace with industry shifts, innovation, and technology.

Practicing law has provided me with a lot of insight and shown me what bumps in the road can do to a family. When the development of a child's creative side yields professional opportunities for him or her—and for some children, a career— helping the child and his or her parent(s) plan or manage a career path for the child and map out an ongoing strategy for the fulfillment of parental responsibilities can be extremely rewarding. When circumstances like these arise, my music lessons and performances from my teen years have paid impressive dividends; those experiences led to a greater appreciation for talented artists, the challenges they face, and the legal assistance I offer. When parents are provided with the right information and resources up front, they often can become their child's most ardent protectors and supporters.

By the way, my husband and I are the proud parents of artistically talented twins who are now college graduates. Their talents have enhanced my 360-degree perspective. Both are musicians. Our son is also pursuing his dream of catching extreme weather on camera, and our daughter remains a gifted songwriter. Their lives have been enriched by the artistic process that has brought to each of them joy, confidence, and hopefully lifelong memories and experiences.

In this book, I emphasize the significance of really knowing your child as well as knowing your child's corresponding limitations and needs. Circumstances that demonstrate a successful working environment for one child can be experienced as failure by another, and knowing which is which for your child is where parents and guardians play a starring role.

I decided to write this book because it didn't exist, and I felt that it was needed. I realized that the combination of all my professional and personal experience had provided me with a unique and valuable perspective to share. When a child is positioned in front of a camera, a microphone, or on a stage in the entertainment industry, the phrase "Child Performer at Work" really does mean just that! I hope this book helps you meet the challenges of making decisions with, and on behalf of, your talented child.

## Parents Defined / Minor Child Defined

Throughout this book, I make reference to parents. I am fully aware that grandparents, aunts, uncles, cousins, other family members, friends, and sometimes legal guardians assume the traditional role of Mom and Dad, but I nonetheless refer only to parents to keep things short and sweet.

I also refer to minors, children, and kids throughout this book. These references generally refer to young people under the age of eighteen, with a few state and union exceptions.

# Important Disclaimer—Please Read Me!

*What you are about to read does not constitute legal or tax advice and should not be relied upon as a substitute for hiring an experienced lawyer and tax professional. Understanding legal precedent and industry customs by consulting a knowledgeable attorney and tax advisor who can properly advise you is very important.*

What you are about to read represents the opinions of the author and may not be applicable to your situation. Circumstances, laws, and regulations may appear similar but may actually be different. Laws, regulations, and industry standards where you live and work impact rulings by courts and arbitrators. Depending on your geographic location, the circumstances, laws, and regulations of your jurisdiction generally dictate what transpires. When it comes to contract breaches in the entertainment industry, especially when children are working, there is virtually no such thing as "one size fits all." Laws and regulations that have been compiled, even upon first publication, may not be complete or up to date and may therefore be inaccurate due to the lapse of time. Moreover, compiled state laws may not include all relevant state laws. Each reader should use caution and discretion in applying any material contained or referenced in this book, including websites, to his or her child's specific circumstance.

# CHAPTER 1

*Considerations for Parents:*
*Children and Commercial Cameras*

Before a parent agrees to place his or her child in front of a commercial camera, it is crucial that he or she first fully weigh the likely benefits, risks, and costs. Making the right decision on behalf of your talented child and considering the impact your choices may have on other family members are steps not to be missed. After all, if a child becomes a commercial success, he or she may lose the normalcy of childhood or even forfeit childhood altogether. Time lost with family and friends cannot be regained. Therefore, it is important to think clearly and dexterously and to seek out and consider as much relevant and reliable information as possible. Doing so may not only be of immense help to a parent in making the decision, but it also is likely to provide comfort. A parent may find relief in realizing that he or she isn't the only one who finds such a decision complicated and difficult. The stakes can be sky-high, so honest assessments are extremely important.

# Crucial Questions for Parents to Consider

- Is your child's talent truly unique and amazing? Do you have sufficient knowledge of what it takes for a child to succeed professionally to make such an assessment? If so, be blunt about your assessment. If not, use your instincts as a starting point, but also consider the opinions of others who may be in a better position to make such an evaluation. For example, have teachers or coaches pulled your child aside for special recognition or roles? Are those teachers and coaches sufficiently trained and accomplished to be in a good position to evaluate your child's talent?

- Does your child seek out and enjoy performing? Your child's comfort level is crucial. He or she must want to be there. Otherwise, your child will be uncomfortable, and it will be a colossal waste of time for everybody else. I can pretty much guarantee that a seven-year-old whose face and body language say, "I am surrounded by old people. This is the last place I want to be!" won't be cast.

- What steps have you taken to enhance your child's skills as a performer? In the book *Outliers* by Malcolm Gladwell, he asserts that "people don't rise from nothing. We do owe something to parentage and patronage."[1] Citing the neurologist Daniel Levitin on a study by K. Anders Ericsson and colleagues on innate talent, Gladwell says that "the striking thing about Ericsson's study is that he and his colleagues couldn't find any 'naturals,' musicians who floated effortlessly to the top while practicing a fraction of the time their peers did. . . . Their research suggests that once a musician has enough ability to get into a top music school, the thing that distinguishes one performer from another is how hard he or she works."[2] Gladwell continues, quoting Levitin: "Ten thousand hours of practice is required to achieve the level of mastery associated with being a world-class expert—in anything. . . . In study after study of composers, basketball players, fiction writers, ice skaters, concert pianists, chess players, master criminals, and what have you, this number comes up again and again. Of course, this doesn't address why some people get more out of their practice sessions than others do."[3] For children, how

...............................................................................

1    Malcolm Gladwell, *Outliers: The Story of Success.* New York: Little Brown & Co., 2008, p. 19.

2    Ibid., p. 39.

3    Ibid., p. 40.

many can master the ten thousand hours in spite of their young age and the relatively few hours they have lived on the planet? "You have to have parents who encourage and support you."[4]

- Are you thinking about moving to pursue your child's dream? Children who live in and around Southern California have greater opportunities to break into the film and television businesses because of their proximity to Los Angeles (LA), a movie-making capital and production hub that includes television.[5] This is generally why parents whose child wants to be a professional performer may split up the family geographically, with one parent moving to LA with the talented child (at least temporarily), while the other stays home to continue working. Alternatively, the entire family picks up to pursue the dream of a film or television career for the child. The legendary Shirley Temple Black, who grew up in Santa Monica, California, wrote reflectively in her autobiography, *Child Star*, "From the day I learned to walk, almost half

........................................................................

4    Ibid., p. 42.

5    A total of 49,296 entertainment work permits were issued by the California Division of Standards and Enforcement from January 1 through December 31, 2014.

of my life had been working in movies. Almost all I knew came from Meglin's Dancing School, eight *Baby Burlesks*, five comedy shorts, six walk-on parts, and one bit part. My earnings were $702.50, but unfortunately my employer was now bankrupt. I was out of a job with no future in sight, and still too young to get into kindergarten. All in all, it was a tough spot for any five-year-old."[6] For those of you who are unfamiliar with this young performer of the 1930s, a very young Shirley Temple was setting the screen on fire with her winning smile and uncanny ability to dance. Her movies topped the US box office, outselling other movies featuring stars such as Clark Gable, Humphrey Bogart, and Greta Garbo.[7]

*Note:* Commercial vibrancy in New York offers substantial opportunities as well, with that state, as the modeling hub, rivaling and outpacing other states. Moreover, states with generous tax credits associated with production, including New York, have experienced a commercial boom, not only for the talent but for production workers and businesses behind the

........................................................................

6   Shirley Temple Black, *Child Star: An Autobiography*. New York: McGraw-Hill, 1988, p. 31.

7   See V. Nathaniel Ang, "Teenage Employment Emancipation and the Law," *Journal of Business Law* 9, no. 2 (2007): 389–419. http://scholarship.law.upenn.edu/jbl/vol9/iss2/5.

camera. Before you fret that your family does not live anywhere near the cities of LA or New York, consider that Louisiana bested California in feature film production in 2013.[8]

Will your child be able to handle rejection? Kids who pursue professional performing careers usually get rejected much more often than they get accepted. If your child really wants a particular role and doesn't get it, will that be okay with him or her? Ask yourself how long you will allow the rejections to continue. Will you give it three months, six months, a year, or more than a year? When you think about egg-timing the rejection process, recall how long a year felt when you were a child. Didn't it feel like an eternity from one birthday to the next? Before you set the egg timer, consider that feeling and also weigh your child's wishes and preferences, temperament, resilience in the face of disappointment, and ability to roll with the punches.

Examine your reasons for wanting to pursue a career for your child as a performer. When you were young, were you talented but deprived of the opportunity to compete as a performer because your parents did not provide you with the lessons and attention you needed or wanted? Has being a star been a lifelong fantasy of yours? Did your parents provide

---

8    See FilmL.A., *2013 Feature Film Production Report*, March 6, 2014.

your older sister or brother with opportunities but leave you out in the process? Dr. Richard N. Wolman, a Harvard Medical School faculty member for more than twenty-five years, is an experienced clinician, teacher, and researcher. As a clinical psychologist with expertise in psychotherapy with individuals, families, and children, he consults regularly with families experiencing divorce. His research focuses on spirituality, child custody, psychotherapy, dreams, and child development.[9] He surmises that when children become extensions of parental aspirations, fears, and dreams, they don't *lose* their identity because they never *had* one. He refers to a parent who lives through his or her child as an "I coulda been a contender" parent and explains that a parent who does this makes sure that the child receives the lessons, time, and devotion the parent missed and is, therefore, more easily blinded by his or her own personal needs. According to Wolman, it turns out that the investments some parents make go beyond money. He says that some parents never cut the umbilical cord emotionally. So the investments made by those parents through their children become emotional, psychic, and fantasy fulfilling for them. That only stops, he has stated, when a parent can enjoy a son or

........................................................................

9    Dr. Wolman's website at www.psychomatrix.com presents much of
     this information.

daughter without viewing the child as an extension of herself or himself.[10]

In the United States we don't need to look very far to see clear and obvious examples of such an intact emotional umbilical cord. Children's participation in recreational sports provides a telling example. Explains Wolman, "Some parents don't care if their kid can sing on key, but they will drive him or her to every soccer match or hockey tryout so that they can show how proficient their child is and he or she can rise to the top and get drafted by college or pro teams."[11] If you speak candidly with referees or umpires who officiate football games for eight- to ten-year-olds (affectionately known by some as "helmet games" because the kids are so small that the regulation football helmet, when worn, makes the child look like a gigantic helmet on two legs), they will tell you about the insanity among certain adults in attendance—be they parents, coaches, or fans. Said one official on a crisp New England day in October, "The coach is screaming at the top of his lungs to a kid to 'Fire off. Shoot the gap and blow him up!'" as if the kid had a clue. This is the same kid who, two weeks later, will dress up in a pirate costume for Halloween and go trick-or-treating. For those parents, you can almost feel that they are the ones who are really on the field

........................................................................

10 Personal interview with Dr. Richard N. Wolman, April 23, 2013.

11 Wolman interview.

or onstage, not their child. They often seem to have little to no appreciation for their child's developmental limitations.

Wolman observes that the new entertainment industry in the United States—which is caught in an epic shift supported by reality television contests—provides parents with the perfect outlet to feed their own needs for attention, fame, and success. "Literally," says Wolman, "these kids are being driven to try-out after tryout after tryout, audition after audition after audition."[12] Denise Simon, a New York City—based acting coach and career consultant who advises parents on the "overcoached" child and how to identify burnout, says, "When I see parents really pushing their child, it drives me absolutely crazy."[13]

The end result of this kind of parenting can get pretty messy, so be thoughtful and candid about your motivation before beginning the process. Here's how:

Let's say that you take out an equity loan on your house for $50,000 so that your son, a budding singer-songwriter, can get into the recording studio with his band and record sixteen original songs. You have to drive about an hour each way to get your son to the studio. Since your son is young, you opt to stay at the studio for hours at a time. You spend money on gas and food. You lose time from work, which costs money, too. You

12    Ibid.

13    Personal interview with Denise Simon, May 5, 2014.

also spend money on guitar and voice lessons, together with the legal fees associated with protecting your son's music. You know that you could probably do some of this work yourself, but you don't want to take the chance that you might mess up the paperwork, so you hire a professional to do it. Eventually, your son's album is finished. You find a company that brokers the music to iTunes and other music sites, and your son's music goes live and viral. Your son and his band decide to perform locally and, eventually, you find yourself driving three to four hundred miles at a time. Two years and $50,000 in the hole later, your son comes to you and drops the bomb. "Mom," he says, "I am not getting along with the band and am especially tired of Matt, the bass guitarist. I'll continue to write songs, but I don't want to be a performer anymore. And I want the band's website taken down, too. I just want to be a normal kid." How would you feel and react to that situation? Would your son's decision be okay with you?

Now change the child performer to a young female gymnast. You and your family have sacrificed significantly toward the goal of her winning Olympic gold—or a medal at the very least. Your family has invested much time and money in this enterprise. They have also had to let go of their wish for the family to stay together. Your daughter trains and boards 2,500 miles from your home, and your younger daughter misses her terribly. Your gymnast daughter comes to you and says that she wants to quit because the coach is mean, the competition has gotten to her, and she is tired of feeling tired. She wants normal friendships and a life beyond the beam. How would you feel and react? Would your daughter's decision be okay? If the answer to that question is either "No" or "I don't know," examine your rationale for wanting to start the process and consider the future sacrifices that you and your family will be making if you do. Dr. Wolman advises that in the course of the child's own development, as she or he begins to evolve a sense of self and pushes back, some parents greatly resist because to them it feels like betrayal (e.g., "After all that your father and I sacrificed for you, you don't want to be a gymnast anymore? Get back out there!").

## *Here's the psychological side of why:*

Dr. Wolman's experience guiding families of divorce makes the tension and impact on kids in demanding and pressure-filled situations, including those in the entertainment industry, all too familiar. Pressure may be placed on the child to achieve a particular result, whether it is in the courts ("I want to live with Mom"), earning a place on an Olympic team, or being cast in a coveted role in a show. "Pressure blinds parental judgment," he says, "and the children are left with the responsibility for their own caretaking and development so they are trying to parent themselves—difficult at best. They become 'parentified,' with some even taking care of their parents. They know too much about money and conflicts and the dark side of interpersonal relationships and anxiety. Some of them do very well at surviving, but they pay the price of precocious development. They lose the opportunity to grow and mature at a reasonable rate because they are catapulted into adulthood. What a child knows about a mortgage, contracts, and sexuality, as examples, are childlike and imperfect, even more imperfect than their parents' view."

## *Here's the practical side of why:*

From personal and professional experience in the entertainment industry, Paul Petersen[14] knows firsthand about the tension of auditions and the impact such auditions have on kids. He became a Mouseketeer on *The Mickey Mouse Club* in the 1950s at age nine and wrote that he became the first ex-Mouseketeer: he was fired for conduct unbecoming.[15] In his teens, he played the much beloved role of Jeff Stone on

14 Born William Paul Petersen in Glendale, California.
15 Paul Petersen, *Walt, Mickey and Me.* New York: Dell, 1977, p. 9.

*The Donna Reed Show*, produced for television in the late 1950s and 1960s, and pretty much grew up during that show's production. He emphasizes that children really don't adjust to the inherent isolation brought on by the competition associated with the audition and casting process. He describes the experience below:

> So there are two rooms. One has two hundred fifty kids in it for a one-day commercial which pays seven hundred fifty dollars. The other room is for the actual audition. Each kid gets four seconds for the audition. The child walks into the audition space, alone, and, speaking from firsthand experience, you give your best but you do it alone. As for me, I didn't want the kids in the outer office to get that job. So the whole structure keeps you isolated. You go to dance school, drama classes, and acting classes. If you are good enough, you are separated out already from your peers because the teachers and coaches know which kids are truly talented.

When asked how he and other children coped, he responded this way:

> Thank God for publicity events. Sometimes we could actually get together apart from our parents by

riddling and other times with gentle deceptions. But kids getting beat up at school for being famous, getting no respect for work that adults performed, and being told to get their butts out of bed because there are a thousand kids who want that job are the facts. In my view, parents are not only deceiving themselves about their family, but they deceive others as well. That having been said, there are children who accept the hard work and rejection for the love of the crowd and the smell of the grease paint.

With that he warned parents to be "hypervigilant when accessing true, real, and prodigious talent for the sake of the children—please!"[16]

## *What can parents do?*

Trust your instincts as your child's mother, father, or guardian. Speak with your child's teachers, coaches, and other trusted advisors who really know your son or daughter well. Gather as much objective information as you can, especially information

16   Personal interview with Paul Petersen, May 20, 2011.

that differs from your own view. The more information and perspective you have, the better.

Understand that I am not talking about parents who encourage their child to keep up with their acting or songwriting workshop, or their voice, guitar, or piano playing, or kids who form garage bands or even girl or boy bands as teens for a "someday" payoff—as long as they stay in school. Perhaps some of these kids will be recognized as winners of prestigious composer or performance awards and scholarships. I don't worry about those kids and their involved parents. One such tyke got on with his life and currently holds a pretty spiffy position as symphony orchestra music director at a prestigious university.

I do worry, though, about the kids who present adorably at a very young age and whose parents sign them up, straightaway, with a model management company. From then on the kids work all the time—commercials, movies, and television—without any normalcy. When they get older, they may be justifiably angry, if not furious, about the hijacking of their childhood. Let's take it a step further. There they sit as twentysomethings. Angry, depressed, and sometimes broke, they surf the Internet and eventually see themselves as first graders in one of their movies. They think wistfully about what other kids were doing back then while they were holed up in a trailer practicing their lines.

So find a long beach, winding road, or tall mountain, and walk along it with your child's other parent, another person entrusted with your child's care, or a trusted friend or advisor before you speak with your son or daughter. If you find yourself walking for two months or even longer, so be it. Of course, your child's preferences are important. If your child does not want the life of a public performer, don't pursue it! Assuming that your child does want that, be mindful that—like the pediatrician, school district, and religious or spiritual education you choose— your child will not be driving to locations for auditions, performances, and other events; that burden will likely fall on you.

As you walk, consider straightforward answers to the following questions:

1. Does my child really want the work?

2. Is my child's talent truly prodigious?

3. Am I an "I coulda been a contender" parent?

4. What are my goals for my child? Are they realistic?

5. Does my child have goals? What are they, and are they realistic?

6. Will my child be able to handle rejection?

7. When will enough be enough? How much rejection will I permit my son or daughter to experience before I open the escape hatch?

8. Will other circumstances, if and as they arise, require me to open the escape hatch? If so, specify those circumstances.

9. Does my child have the ability to handle stress and pressure? What support structures are in place to help my child along the way?

10. How will such a decision affect my family? Am I ready to leave my other children, and perhaps a spouse, to hit the road with my prodigious son or daughter? Have I made arrangements for my other children at home? How will their needs be met? Assuming that I am ready to leave my other children behind, have I thought about how that decision will affect their relationships with me and with their sister or brother? If I am married or have a partner, how will such a decision affect him or her?

11. Is my child willing to forgo birthday parties, Friday night football games, and other social experiences for the experience of potentially performing at a professional level? Will my child feel drafted, indentured, and gypped out of a normal childhood once she or he understands and experiences the loss?

12. Am I willing to give up my own everyday experiences, and in some instances employment, in order to help my son or daughter with this goal?

13. What will I do with the money my child can bring into the family?

14. Can our family financially swing the commitment without our child's earnings? (If so, map that out.) If not, what percentage will I require? Am I prepared to money map what I spend and to collect verifiable and legible receipts along the way? (*Note:* Consult a trusted accountant who can help you plan. If you do not know one, ask people you trust to make a recommendation. See Chapter 11, "Taxes—Especially for Parents.")

15. What precautions can my family and I take to avoid a financial or emotional crash? What precautions can I take to make sure that the experience doesn't result in my child eventually feeling betrayed or broken or being broke?

## *Precautions for Parents*

Make your son or daughter's life as normal as possible. As described in greater detail in Chapter 5, "Education," meet with your child's school principal, teachers, and even the superintendent of the school district to determine how your child's educational requirements can be met. Look for any flexibility offered by the school system, and get creative within the confines of educational requirements. Companies like On Location Education, an educational consulting service for young performers, can be of crucial importance when families remain committed to their son's or daughter's ongoing education. Says Alan Simon, On Location Education president, "If you choose to put your child in the entertainment industry, it affects everything they do. Ultimately, it is the child who wants the career. It is the kid dragging the parent to the door. But the parent must understand what it means, how deeply involved in both aspects [performing and education] the parents have to be and how it affects the parent at home. And the siblings left at home."[17]

When asked if children are able to assess the wear and tear the business will have on them, Simon's opinion was a resounding "No." Commit yourself to helping your child retain his or her friendships and to learning to tell the difference between new authentic friends and followers who want, for a variety of reasons, to get close. Bend over backward to keep those friendships healthy. If your child is a teen, communications by text and tweet to trusted friends will, hopefully, continue. But

---

17   Personal interview with Alan Simon, January 22, 2010.

educate your child about the important distinction between friends and fans. Pay generous and ongoing attention to those connections and activities, especially if your son's or daughter's success through athletics or entertainment becomes evident. A painfully unattractive side of attention paid to star kids is that their stardom can evoke bullying and other cruelties—cyber or otherwise—instigated by friends and acquaintances who are envious. So be hypervigilant, respond to signs of stress or withdrawal, and help your son or daughter work through it. Support groups for current and former child performers and their parents exist. (See Chapter 13, "Website Support.") Finally, be aware of how a child's stardom may affect any siblings he or she has. A new social order could emerge in your family as a direct result of your child's success. Writes the late Shirley Temple Black, "Brother Jack had the misfortune . . . to take a swipe at my passing bottom over some petty frustration. Summoned by one indignant yowl, Mother boxed his ears and forbade him ever to strike at me again under threat of a worse thrashing for him. From that instant on Jack recognized a new social order in our household. His sister was his mother's pet project. When it came to an argument with me, he was bound to lose."[18]

..........................................................................

18    Black, *Child Star*, p. 59.

# CHAPTER 2

*Want to Be Famous, Kid?*
*Tips for Parents and Avoiding Scams*

The rearview mirror of parenting offers parents a pretty clear view of what they did right—but also what they could have done differently or better. Whether or not a child can sing or dance, act like a pro, excel as an athlete, or otherwise perform in ways reserved for a tiny number of children, such parental assessment tends to unite parents. Moreover, parenting styles may mellow with experience (and sheer exhaustion), so much so that the older children in a family might be driven crazy as they watch, green with envy, their baby brother or sister "get away with murder." In contrast, they may recall their early years as choked with chores, responsibilities, and curfews while their siblings got to do whatever they wanted! Now consider parents of children working in "the business."

One of the premier challenges that unite parents new to the business, whether or not they live in areas densely populated with entertainment and sports companies, centers on the lack of credible information from veteran parents. Naturally, parents with experience navigating the terrain may know what to expect and have greater dexterity handling challenges as they arise. So I imagined that it would be helpful, and pretty easy, to persuade parents of child performers or athletes to look back on their experiences and offer advice. Boy, was I ever wrong—talk about a touchy subject!

Many of the experienced parents I called couldn't get me off the phone fast enough. It became quite an undertaking to get meaningful discussions going about what parents felt they had done right, let alone about where they felt they had made missteps or blunders. Even people who I have known for quite some time preferred not to talk. One parent explained, "No way, Sally. My kid is so angry with me that he'd never speak with me again if I talked to you." Guaranteeing complete anonymity provided little comfort.

It's understandable why some parents may feel this way. Some young performers, particularly as they get older or become adults, believe they were cheated out of a childhood and unfairly drafted as breadwinners because of their talent. They may feel that the commercial Ferris wheel ought not to have been powered by their labor and the losses that came with it. Years later, they may still feel angry. The lingering and festering anger felt by children about their parents for allowing these losses to occur can come back to haunt parents. Somehow, when commercial opportunities arise that place kids' strengths and weaknesses front and center, parents' time-honored defensive role of shielding and sheltering their children can be forgotten. This is why it is important that parental consent be granted only when the focus is on the child, and the decision truly is in the child's best interest. Inflamed and unaddressed feelings can be life changing for an entire family, including the children left at home, prompting some parents to instinctively or defensively run for cover from prying eyes.

Nevertheless, some parents were willing to talk. The following list cobbles together comments, ruminations, and experiences of parents whose children work or worked in at least one of the businesses comprising the entertainment industry. I have added, with some creative editing, circumstances taken from my practice, too. The list is intended to help parents in similar circumstances. Do-over remarks are provided for added perspective alongside featured remarks by Paul Petersen. For everyone's protection, all indicia of identity are omitted.

- I should not have pulled my kid out of school.

  *Do-over:*

  Education and the socialization that come with attending school, both inside and outside of the classroom, are hard to replace over time. Since financial stability and the entertainment industry are not twin souls, your child will need his or her education. Make sure that you fight to protect it.

- I shouldn't have spent $8,000 on a modeling program. That was a waste of money. My daughter lost time away from her friends and older sisters, and my husband and I found ourselves struggling at the grocery store.

*Do-over:*

Allow a young person to experience or test-drive the casting process before committing to a long-term ride. Locate either a reputable modeling or talent agency interested in working with and advising your child or an experienced agent willing to bring him or her into the fold.

- I did not ask for or check references. Afterward, I was embarrassed.

*Do-over:*

References, references, references. Ask for them before you decide who is best suited and sufficiently experienced to work with your child. Also, learn who owns the company that is courting your son or daughter. If the company is local, a good way to find this out is to navigate the secretary of state's office in your state. If the company is not local, ask where the company principally does business and then go to that state's secretary of state office (e.g., if it is a New York company, then go to the New York secretary of state's office). You might be surprised at how much information can be found online. While you are at it, navigate the state attorney general's office, too.

Some sites that might prove helpful as first stops include www.minorcon.org, www.onlocationeducation.com, www .childreninfilm.com, and www.bizparentz.org. (Also see Chapter 13, "Website Support.") You may find additional websites that are useful, so don't forget to do your homework. The mission, substance, approach, and style of each company might be as unique as its respective founders.

Paul Petersen started A Minor Consideration—a nonprofit, tax-deductible foundation formed to give guidance and support to young performers—after a friend, a former child star, ended his life on January 19, 1990. They were the same age. Petersen explains, "On that day, I vowed that it will never happen again. If a kid actor is in trouble, the personal guilt will kill me if I don't intervene."[19] So A Minor Consideration was born. Keeping his word, Petersen has provided unwavering support as a child advocate who continues to help countless former

........................................................

19    Petersen interview.

stars who have struggled. Many have embraced sobriety under his umbrella. A proven platinum standard for child advocacy spanning two decades and counting, Petersen's personal knowledge of the workings of the industry and his passion to make a real difference for young performers (past, present, and future) and their families have made him a one-of-a-kind, incomparable trailblazer. In addition, his collaborative support with many others helped change the law in California, resulting in that state having the most comprehensive set of laws in the nation addressing child performers. The law, in part, spells out clearly that money earned belongs to the young performer and that 15 percent of gross earnings must be placed in trust for the minor until age eighteen. (Also see Chapter 8, "And the Money Belongs to . . .")

My advice is that you should spend plenty of time with the details of these websites. Get as much information as you can until you feel yourself overloaded. Then get up the next day and do it all over again, until you feel that you are retaining sufficient information to apply your knowledge to your child or circumstance. Your child is depending on you to steer the ship. In order to do that, you need to know where you are going, what to do when you get there, and who is trustworthy. So give yourself the time you need to acclimate.

Chinese star athlete Yao Ming provides an interesting analogy. He first donned his National Basketball Association (NBA) uniform for the Houston Rockets on October 30, 2002, and has since retired from the game. Setting aside sponsor accolades for Yao serving as a human "gateway for the Asian market . . . the NBA symbol for globalization,"[20] Yao's experience is instructive. He compared the challenge of playing basketball in America to trying to learn a foreign language. He emphasized that time to adjust was needed by team members and noted that "no matter whether you are new or an old team member, you need time to adjust to one another."[21] So if Ming, who was born in Shanghai, China, can travel the globe to play in Houston, Texas, mastering strikingly different cultures, languages, and the professional NBA along the way, adaptation to the US entertainment or sports industry is achievable. So let's move on with that list of experiences to watch out for parents of young talent:

- A Halloween scene was being filmed—in the dark, of course. The costume trailer was in the woods. A

---

20  Ben Keeler and John Nauright, "Team Yao: Yao Ming, the NBA, Sporting Goods and Selling Sport to China," *American Journal of Chinese Studies* 12, no. 2 (2005): 203–218.

21  Dana Milbank, "Washington Sketch: Sports-Loving President Finds It's Not Always Fun and Games," *Washington Post*, July 28, 2009, www.washingtonpost.com/wp-dyn/content/article/2009/07/27/AR2009072702527.html.

production assistant told the young child, "Just walk back to the set," but did not provide an escort. The kid, scared to death, got lost.

*Do-over:*

Don't let your child out of your sight or earshot. (But be pleasant and respectful of the working environments of others.) Would you drop off your four-year-old at the mall to be cared for by a stranger? Just because a production assistant works on a movie set where kids are working does not necessarily mean that he or she comes up aces in the common sense department or knows how to best work with kids.

- I should have found parents who did this before and asked them how much it would cost before I started spending money.

*Do-over:*

In the future, contact organizations that can lead you to parents who have been in your position. Research articles about kids who are already working as performers. Ask family and friends to forward any relevant articles that they come across. Often, at least one parent will be on-site for the audition process or at the performance venue to be within sight or earshot of the working child. Keep in mind that most young performers don't have a driver's license. Mom or Dad will need to drive them to auditions, practices, performances, and so on.

- I let my nine-year-old son call the shots. I thought I was being a good mom giving him his dream. Honestly, I had a hard time saying no to him.

*Do-over:*

No isn't the hardest word to say. I counsel my clients, whether they are performers, parents, or employers, that the word *no* is one of the most powerful and influential words in the English language and that they should get used to saying it. How the word is said makes the impact.

- We spent way too much money on travel costs to California—and for what? Instead of my son being one talented kid out of a hundred, he was one out of a thousand.

*Do-over:*

By first researching local opportunities in your own state and neighboring states, you help your child by introducing him or her to the commercial work site without leaving behind his or her familiar life and friends. By doing so, you also avoid the inevitable investment of money and time—not to mention the disruption—that occurs when you pack up and move. Decisions about the pursuit of a dream for a child should be made carefully, strategically, and methodically. Be mindful that some families elect to split up. One parent stays behind to work, pay bills, and manage the rest of the family, while the other parent and child are hundreds or thousands of miles away on location or pursuing opportunities. This can be hard on everyone, and it is time lost that can never be regained. So please choose wisely and take a thoughtful approach to your child's professional development.

Consider local opportunities such as drama or music workshops, after-school programs, and camps designed to nurture young talent that emphasize performing and creative arts. Offer your child the chance to experience his or her artistic evolution and growth. Allow him or her to experience what performing publicly feels like over a period of time. Don't rush. If your child wants to be in media now, start with your child at your local public library to research, online and offline, local talent agencies and modeling companies that may lead to opportunities for being cast in commercial advertisements. Print advertising options generally come first before television and other media, although some online sponsorships might crop up. Similarly, states with tax incentive programs bring in film production that may lead to casting calls for young extras. (Extras are people typically cast to create background for a scene.) Entities adept at working with young people and their parents are generally available in cities tied to commercial markets. If you live in a remote area, prospective opportunities through the casting call process may be available through regional market agencies and companies in cities geographically closer to you.

Be mindful that online reputations and associated credibility leading to bona fide business credibility must be vetted.

- My son wanted to be famous, but he didn't want to work like a grown-up to get there.

*Do-over:*

Explain to your son or daughter that fame is not a destination. Even in situations where performers work incredibly hard for years, there is no guarantee that recognition, fame, or financial rewards will result. In fact, sometimes some or all of these can be utterly and frustratingly elusive.

- I wanted to be a famous mother and pushed my kid.

*Do-over:*

The talent and passion to perform must originate in the child. It's not fair to a child to push him or her into performing when the pursuit is really about proving your relevance or fulfilling your dream. This can lead to great unhappiness for everyone involved, so for the sake of your child and yourself, avoid doing it.

- It took me years to appreciate how my daughter's loss of privacy and loneliness affected her. I overlooked the warning signs of her stress and strain because of her talent. At the time, I felt the ends justified the means.

*Do-over:*

Remember that being a parent means providing your child with the protection he or she needs. Anticipating the isolation by taking steps, beforehand, to combat the likelihood of such feelings can go a long way. Schedule online games or Skype conversations to keep friendships close. And always keep a cell phone or other mobile device fully charged.

- I identified my daughter's prodigious talent as a songwriter. Tens of thousands of dollars and one album later, she figured out that performing "solo" wasn't for her. Then the bottom fell out of the record business. But here's the funny thing: I don't regret it. It's a phenomenal album, shows the world her God-given talents, and has done wonders for her self-esteem. Her fans continue to listen to her songs and to say how happy the songs make them. Hopefully, established artists will hear her songs, want to sing them, and perhaps some of the money spent will ultimately be recouped. The bottom line is that I wrote the checks, not my daughter, and for that, I take full responsibility. *Do-over:*

Hindsight is 20/20. It is laudable that responsibility has been taken for an expensive lesson learned.

For touring musicians, public performance is an integral part of the job. So before big money is spent on production and recording, offer the young performer as much public performance time as possible through open microphone nights, school and charitable performances, and events tied to fund-raisers. One of my young and more industrious performers busted a piggy bank with money earned from playing out at sweet sixteen and bar/bat mitzvah parties.

Admittedly, what can be frustrating for parents is the preference of some music managers and publishers to listen to "radio-ready" hits for their artists to consider covering. With the advancement of technology, production costs have declined and some talented youngsters are wisely learning how to use the tools necessary for music production. (This would be the silver lining.) Still, if a parent decides to hire an exceptional producer to bring a child's music to the next level, that investment would typically be paid by parents and likely viewed as a loan to be repaid later from sales. The expectation for recoupment is best shared with the young performer when the parent determines that the child is mature enough to understand the difference between a parent's ordinary support obligation and five-figure production costs.

· I have a daughter who was in a girl band. One of the other mothers was really pushy. I felt that I was being bossed around. It was awful. I was afraid to say anything for fear of making trouble for my daughter. To this day, I don't know what I should have done.

*Do-over:*

This situation is common. Sometimes one parent will jump in because that is his or her personal style. At other times, one parent will seize the opportunity to fill a hole that needs plugging. If speaking directly with the parent who is making life miserable is not an option, let the band's manager or attorney know the situation and ask for assistance. Experienced professionals should know how to approach and resolve that typical commercial occurrence.

- I should have trusted my gut and said no to a "manager" who demanded $5,000 to make my son "a star."

*Do-over:*

Reputable managers and other professionals don't do that. California law prohibits talent representatives from doing it. (See the "Scams" section in this chapter.)

- If someone pressures you and your child to sign an agreement "right now," say no.

*Do-over:*

Take the time to read over an agreement in order to fully understand it. Consider hiring a lawyer or other professional who can explain it to you. Don't be intimidated by print. Both parties may agree to add or subtract language.

Consider this comment: "My wife and I did something ingenious. We got a lawyer and followed his advice."

- I used my son's earnings to pay tuition for my daughter—his sister—to attend private school. At the time, I thought it made sense because his father and I were supporting him. He is very angry now and won't come home for the holidays.

*Do-over:*

Save all or as much of your child's money as possible for your child, and keep receipts.

· Since my daughter was nine years old, she wanted to be a "cover girl." When she was sixteen, I drove her to New York City. One of the account managers at the agency who offered her an opportunity to model promised to put her up in an apartment and take care of her. I dropped her belongings off, and we said our good-byes. Suffice it to say that it didn't work out. The agency ran her ragged with auditions, and when she called home, I was really concerned. She sounded exhausted. When I asked her what was going on, she wouldn't tell me, but I could tell she was crying and it scared me.

*Do-over:*

Do not send your teenage son or daughter to New York City, or any other city, alone and without either your supervision or someone close to you, to "make it" in the modeling business. He or she may literally starve, and few teens (and frankly few grown-ups) are ready for the challenges that they may face in pursuit of such a goal. As you will discover, a 2013 New York law now mandates supervision for young models at work.

Finally, here's a riddle for you:

What do a mall, a self-described "marketing specialist," and paying for expensive photographs have to do with seriously making it in the entertainment industry?

Answer: Not much.

## Scams

Businesses have cropped up like dandelions to fuel the demand for kid commercial placements, especially now because of the growth in programming for children and teens. The focus on mainstream kids who are nothing more than adorable or "the right fit" stands in sharp contrast to developing star kids born with a prodigious talent who have spent mega hours crafting it. A specific example of the latter is classical crossover singer Jackie Evancho. She was a contestant on *America's Got Talent* at age ten and created several albums of music with lightning speed. Also consider, more broadly, the roving numbers of child cast members of former and current Broadway shows and their touring companies. The sheer athleticism required of those working performers not only means star talent but also dogged determination and stamina.

The growth of Disney's Media Networks catering to kids and family, Discovery Family (formerly Discovery Kids and the Hub Network), Nickelodeon (Nick, Jr.), and other kid-focused media has resulted in greater demand for young talent and an ongoing supply of young hopefuls. "When international pop star Justin Bieber can get discovered by uploading a few grainy clips of himself to YouTube, kids from every corner of the country feel that they, too, can catch their big break."[22] Sadly, scammers know this.

Presentations in malls, radio commercials, and even small ads in newspapers or online may attract kids to show up for an audition, and voilà, like magic, they'll be pulled onto a stage, into an aspiring modeling or music career, and hoisted upward and onward to the big time. Not so fast . . . If you have a child who is lured by such marketing tactics, this is probably as good a time as any to teach him or her that if something sounds too good to be true, it probably is too good to be true.

........................................................................

22  Neil Swidey, "What Does It Take to Become a Disney Star?" *Boston Globe Magazine*, May 27, 2012, www.bostonglobe.com/2012/05/26/actingyoung/gaXPr6Ys86ginVMlHzV0IO/story.html.

So how does a parent spot a scam? According to Denise Simon, the "7 Signs of a Casting Scam" include the following promises:[23]

1. **I can make you a star.** Legitimate casting directors and agents see promise and potential in their clients, but they do not make grand promises of stardom, especially on the first or second meeting. Their websites also do not glamorize the life of an actor. They know that acting is a tough business. There are no guarantees, even when the actor is talented and has great looks.

2. **Earn up to $300 per day as an extra.** If it sounds too good to be true, it probably is. A background actor "extra" makes $148 per day in LA County. Non-union jobs typically pay much less.

3. **"Don't stop believing."** Inspirational messages are meant to lure people who are desperate for success and have little experience in the acting industry. Legitimate agencies look for confident, successful, and poised talent. Sure, they want actors with big

.................................................................

23  Denise Simon, "7 Signs of a Casting Scam," *Backstage*, October 24, 2013, www.backstage.com/advice-for-actors/backstage-experts/7-signs-casting-scam. Reprinted with permission.

dreams, but they don't specifically advertise for actors who are down-and-out.

4.  **Rush casting calls and immediate auditions.** Representatives . . . in a rush are often trying to close the deal. They know that people tend to make poor decisions under pressure and are more likely to make a payment for some legitimate-sounding purpose. Legitimate casting directors occasionally cast last minute; however, they generally require you to submit a headshot and résumé well before they invite you to an interview or audition.

5.  **Casting call ads on Craigslist.** A recent Craigslist advertisement in the New York City area displayed the NBC logo and claimed to be casting for extras on a new TV series. Don't believe it! Established production companies in urban areas use established casting directors to provide extras for their upcoming shows. Those companies do not advertise on Craigslist, in classified ads, or through representatives stopping people in a shopping mall.

6.  **"All types, ages, and ethnicities wanted."** Specific roles generally require a specific look, age, ethnicity, or type. Be suspicious when almost anyone could fit into the advertised opportunity.

7. **Major casting director accepting calls until 10:00 p.m.** Major casting directors never hide their identities. Neither do they have operators standing by to take your call late into the night. Sketchy and suspect contact information is a big tip-off to a scam. Do not call companies that provide a telephone number with no other identifying information.

In California, the Krekorian Scam Prevention Act[24] forbids talent representatives from charging fees to clients in exchange for the promise of securing employment, so companies who do business that way may hit the road and set up "shop" in other states. If confronted by a company representative whose left hand offers promises of Hollywood fame and a shiny brochure as the right hand reaches for your money, keep walking.

## Considerations for Parents: Summary

Keep your child enrolled in school. Be objective when assessing your child's talent. Honesty about your motivations cannot be overemphasized. Do not place your child in front of a

---

24 Named after Paul Krekorian, a former Democratic State Assembly majority leader who went on to serve on the Los Angeles City Council.

camera because that is what *you* want. Learn as much as you can about the industry. Do your homework by researching industry resources and networks. Go to websites designed to support you and your child (see Chapter 13, "Website Support"), and read the information on those websites. You needn't agree with all the opinions that are expressed, or believe all the information that is presented, in order to formulate your own educated views on the information provided.

Watch your money. In the entertainment industry, you don't have to pay very much to have your child involved. Assuming your child has the passion, ability, and commercial traits being sought, you can get by with an inexpensive headshot. Do your homework and get references when building your child's team. Find a person you trust and respect who is involved in the business, and ask that person for a recommendation. Locate other parents whose children are involved or were involved in the industry. You might be able to identify such parents in published stories featuring other kids. Contact companies who serve as references for the integrity of other companies. Check online reviews with the caveat that you are seeking the opinion of nameless people or entities whose motivations for writing the recommendations remain unknown to you.

If your son or daughter is passionately interested in pursuing—for example—acting and is older, contemplate plunking down your available cash in a college fund for higher education specializing in drama and the arts. If your child is younger and passionate about drama or music, consider a local drama or music workshop, after-school program, or camp recommended by other parents or by your child's school. If your son or daughter loves to dance, find a studio, gym, academy, or school that suits your child. If your child desperately wants commercial work—for example, a hot dog commercial—and you have been worn down by his or her begging, look for work in your home state or as close to your home state as possible. Get a seasoned professional, such as an agent or attorney, to explain what a contract says before you sign it. Do not allow someone to pressure you into signing when you're not ready. That goes double for your child. Negotiations do occur. Remember that the company or entity who hired the person to hand you the paperwork to sign probably hired an attorney or experienced business pro to advance and protect its interests. Finally, and again, if an opportunity appears too good to be true, trust your instincts and walk the other way.

# CHAPTER 3

*Tricks of the Trade*

*Disclaimer:* As stated at the beginning of this book, laws and industry standards where you live and work affect rulings by courts and arbitrators. Your child's circumstances and the laws of your jurisdiction generally dictate what transpires. So what you are about to read is no substitute for the advice of a seasoned and experienced attorney. Now, on with the show.

A seasoned legislator once told me that you can't legislate human behavior. How right he was. Ah, humans! Put up a legal barrier, and plots and plans to end-run the law will eventually crop up like dandelions. Just ask any copyright lawyer whose clients supported his or her family—once upon a time—with record sales, radio airplay, and licensing. With the advent of downloadable singles and peer-to-peer file sharing, music sales plummeted. Fans no longer had to buy the entire album to get the one song they'd heard on the radio. Frankly, and technically, they didn't need to buy the one song either.

The law was easily circumvented, triggering immense changes for musicians and the music industry.

Over the years, and particularly now due to the significant uptick in the number of children in front of commercial cameras, hurdle jumping and end-running continue to take on new forms. For example, companies can jam parents' to-do lists with obligations traditionally assumed by a manager or make the parent a party to the contract. This lightens the manager's workload, reduces the manager's costs, and lowers the risk of a child's disaffirmance (i.e., legally walking away from a signed contract) by requiring a parent to guarantee a son's or daughter's performance and obliging them to pay for the farm, so to speak, if the child walks away. (See Chapter 9, "How Kids Get Out of Contracts: Disaffirmance" for more information.)

A few details should add some perspective. Consider the sage assessment of veteran music lawyer and specialist Donald Passman. According to Passman, the most important aspects of the manager's job are as follows:

1. Helping you with major business decisions
2. Helping you with the creative process
3. Promoting your career
4. Assembling your professional team
5. Coordinating your concert tours

6. Pounding your record company to maximize the advertising and marketing campaigns for your records

7. Generally, being a buffer between you and the outside world[25]

# *Working with Contracts*

## *Being Treated Fairly*

A common music industry practice is for managers to invest in the careers of their young artists and pay for costs and expenses associated with the musician's artistic development. If and when the money comes in, those managers get paid back, plus they are paid an agreed-upon commission.

Keep this in mind as you consider the following vignettes. The stories have been tweaked to protect identities and corresponding circumstances. Names are fictitious and do not relate to any real person, company, or entity. Please be aware as you read that varied state laws and the corresponding public

................................................................

25   Donald S. Passman, *All You Need to Know About the Music Business*, 8th ed. New York: Free Press, 2012, pp. 28–29. Passman's book is an excellent primer to read before you and your child head out for the music business.

policies of those states can have a substantial impact on court rulings or settlements.

A fifteen-year-old teen who sings, dances, and writes his own music comes to see me with his parents and a personal management contract in hand. Like others who have come to my office, they want to know if the contract is a good deal. Lawyers who have the right measure of education, training, and experience understand that recommending a deal under circumstances that they would not accept themselves may be a professional hazard.

As I began to read this particular management agreement, what jumped out at me was the management company's decision to make the parents a party to the contract along with their son. When I pointed this out to the father, he told me that the company owners made no secret of their deep resentment of lawyers and courts. Mimicking the company president's deep, husky voice, he said, "No way are we going to pay for a court process and lawyers to protect us." *Translation: The legislature creates a law that protects investors who contract with kids, and the governor signs it into law. Parents, guardians, or even companies (in select states) may file a petition with the court, seeking the court's contract approval. Once a judge approves the contract, the minor cannot walk away from what that contract obligates him or her to do.*

But certain investors, like the president of the company in this story, feel that the process is a waste of their resources (time and money).

Now, allow me to give you a sense of this particular contract. It required the parents to

- pay the manager a commission equal to 25 percent of their son's gross earnings forever if, for whatever reason, the manager does not receive his commission directly and forever;
- do all the driving;
- pay all the travel costs;
- pay all of the manager's costs associated with managing their son, including the costs of the manager's travel;
- repay any of the manager's loans related to their son's career promptly;
- pay all fees associated with their son's vocal training, choreography, and wardrobe;
- guarantee their son's performance;
- assume all risks associated with their son's performance, and pay all losses to the management company and any other companies claiming damages if their son doesn't abide by the arrangement

> (the latter, in some form, may be included in a typical parent agreement or release); and
>
> • pay all fees associated with making the contract enforceable, making it the parents' responsibility to pay to have the management company protected.

Based on your newfound knowledge, does this contract strike you as fair? If you think it might be okay because the manager's connections could lead the young singer to his big break, consider this: even assuming that all of those obligations might be acceptable in your view, could these parents afford them? If the answer to that last question is "No," but the parents sign the agreement anyway, be mindful of what may likely follow. Parents who sign contracts of this type may legally place their wallets in play (depending, of course, upon the facts of the case and their state's laws). Therefore, if their son or daughter eventually disaffirms the contract and walks away, the management company will undoubtedly look to the underage performer and/or his parents for payment and reimbursement for commissions on whatever money the child artist generated and earned. Simply put, the management company will seek to be made whole for the work it did by requiring the performer and/or his parents to pay back what it claims to have lost. (See Chapter 10, "Parent Agreements.")

So what does the manager receive if a deal like this gets signed but not approved by the court? The manager gets a claim, at the very least, in the form of a lawsuit against the young performer and/or his or her parent or parents.

Each state has its own brand of legal claims. At its core, breach of contract claims generally include requests for damages including, for example, actual and projected commissions, expense reimbursements, associated legal fees, and even reasonable expenses. Clearly, it is important to be mindful.

Some states, depending on what state laws dictate, may offer protection to young performers and their families in a circumstance like the one just described. Thus, based on particular facts, a state court judge could dismiss the manager's claims, leaving the manager empty-handed.

Consider this next scenario:

Joe and June are raising their son, Michael, who is fifteen, a sophomore in high school, and a killer bass player. Unbeknownst to them, Michael enters an online contest and gets "discovered" by a music production company. The prize he wins includes having one song produced by an award-winning producer. The company forwards a production contract to Michael's parents, which they must sign in order for him to accept the prize. Since the family business is farming, they have no knowledge of the music industry or of music contracts. They ask around, and eventually, a corporate lawyer known by one of their friends refers them to a music lawyer. They are relieved to find someone who knows the business.

The music lawyer agrees to represent Michael's interests by reading the contract and amending it so that the terms are fair. He quotes them a pretty reasonable rate for his legal services, and away they go. Since Joe and June understandably want to save money on legal fees, however, they decide to stop the legal meter by taking the revisions Michael's lawyer proposed after he reviewed the draft contract and delivering them to the company themselves. Interestingly, the company's rep looks over the revisions and says, "These changes look fine. I'll have my personal assistant make the changes and send the revised draft to you." He does what he promised to do. The revisions written by the lawyer hired by Joe and June make it into the next draft, whereupon the producer's rep says, "Since Michael will be at the recording studio Saturday morning, I'll bring the final contract with me and see all of you then." Relying on the rep's promise, Joe and June show up with

Michael, and Michael signs the final contract. His parents sign an acknowledgment.

Unfortunately, the contract Michael signed and which his parents acknowledged was the original contract and not the revised one.

Was this an honest mistake or an unfair and deceptive trade practice?

Whatever you call it, the event was not discovered for over a year. Contract copies were filed away, and no courtesy copy was sent to Michael's lawyer (who would likely have made the discovery much sooner). So what happened next? When the error was realized, Michael's lawyer made it crystal clear that, although the mistake might have been an honest one, in the event that an adequate settlement could not be worked out extricating Michael from the company, the matter would be made public. The company agreed to pay Joe and June's "reasonable" legal fees to work out a fair settlement.

### The Other Side of the Coin

Now, let's place ourselves in the company's shoes for greater perspective.

A small management company, let's call it Management Co., agrees to sign Justin, a fourteen-year-old aspiring actor, to a personal management contract. Justin's mother and father sign a parent agreement (see Chapter 10, "Parent Agreements"), essentially guaranteeing their son's performance and agreeing to pay the company for whatever losses it sustains if the deal goes south. Through the dedicated efforts of one special manager at Management Co., Justin's talents are honed. He snags a few small roles and finally secures a pretty big break on a weekly TV show. Justin receives the exciting news a few weeks before his eighteenth birthday. That's when the roof caves in on Management Co. Justin decides to disaffirm the contract with Management Co. over his manager's strenuous pleas not to do "this crazy thing." Justin dreams about what he can do with the 15 percent he would otherwise be spending to pay this manager. Understandably, Justin's manager is devastated and terribly hurt. So much time and energy went into crafting Justin's big break, and the manager genuinely cared about Justin and his family. Eventually, Management Co.'s owner talked Justin's now former manager into supporting an action (lawsuit) against Justin (and his parents) for unpaid commissions.

The company eventually prevailed. Due expressly to the efforts and time invested by Justin's manager, the benefits Justin received from the management contract were undeniable. Although Justin could walk away because he was a minor at the time the agreement was signed (and a court had not approved the arrangement), the company would be made whole under a legal theory known as *quantum meruit* (pay for the services provided). Justin's parents upheld their guarantee and indemnified Management Co. They paid the commissions owed to Justin's former manager, plus Management Co.'s legal fees and expenses. *Ouch.*

Here is another example from a management company's perspective:

Sam's mom gives consent to Ed, a professional photographer, to take photographs of then eleven-year-old Sam, a young model. The underage model receives a few hundred dollars for a two-hour photo session. He is photographed in a variety of poses. There is no nudity and nothing risqué about any of the shots taken. Sam's mother signs a release and an acknowledgment that Ed owns the photographs and that he can use them in any way he wishes, including selling or licensing them to anyone, including to a company. A few years later, one of the photographs surfaces in a series of print commercials. Sam's mom sees one of her son's photographs in a magazine while she waits for services at a local hair salon. Upset, she calls the company using the photograph of her son. The company manufactures and distributes food that, in the mom's words, "My son wouldn't be caught dead eating." Sam's mom makes several phone calls and sends some e-mails. She finally tracks down the person who licensed the photograph for the advertisement. She also requests a copy of the written release that supposedly gave the company permission to use the photograph. Sure enough, by e-mail she receives a copy of the photographer's release that she signed. She recognizes her signature and remembers when she signed it. She then takes the steps to seek a court ruling to stop the use of the photograph in the advertisement. In the end, the ruling favored the company financially.

The judge would not allow Sam to disaffirm a release signed by his mother.[26]

Before I get into the next story, here's the quick and dirty on option and purchase agreements. Such arrangements are a standard way of doing business in the entertainment industry. An option and purchase agreement can give a person (or a company) the opportunity to do something—commonly, to buy a story or book—without the obligation to actually make or produce it. It is common that when an option period begins, the prospective buyer makes a payment. That entitles the prospective buyer to undertake preproduction or production activities, such as prepare and submit treatments or screenplays based on the story or book.

Now, on with the narrative involving an aspiring writer and her mom. This story cuts both ways.

Molly, a sixteen-year-old writer, completes her first novella. Her mother knows someone who knows

---

26  See *Shields v. Gross*, 58 N.Y. 2d 338 (1983), which ruled similarly more than thirty years ago. But the dissenting judge in that case (the judge who disagreed with the way the case was ultimately decided) noted that "it has long been the rule in this state [New York] that a minor enjoys an almost absolute right to disaffirm a contract entered into by either the minor or the minor's parent on behalf of the minor." That dissent was cited in a more recent 2007 case that upheld a seventeen-year-old minor's right to disaffirm a management contract.

someone, and eventually Molly's mom receives an e-mail with an attachment for an option and purchase of her daughter's novella. A production company wants to use the novella as the foundation for a made-for-TV movie.

Molly's mom sends back both copies of the contract after signing for herself and for her daughter by signing Molly's name. The option period begins, and a check for $5,000 arrives. The check is made out to Molly. On the back of the check, Molly's mom writes "For Deposit Only" and deposits the funds into her (the mom's) bank account.

Molly's mom spends the money, primarily on clothes for herself as well as an expensive spa weekend for herself and a friend. Later, she says she fully intended to pay back the money.

A few months later, Molly overhears her mother on the phone talking about the option agreement and explaining the circumstances. She flies into an explosive rage. Talk about feelings of betrayal! Molly did not want her novella to be made into a TV movie. She wanted it published as a book. Period.

So what happened after that? Once the company learned that Molly had not signed her name to the contract or the check and had not received a single penny binding the deal, Molly and the company held the legally necessary facts to substantiate dueling complaints against Molly's mother for fraud and other assorted legalities stemming from misrepresentation and bad faith. The company agreed to pass on the project (no made-for-TV movie), which gave Molly what she wanted. Molly's mom agreed to repay the fees to the company, plus half of the cost of the attorney's fees the company had incurred, which is what the company wanted. Settlement discussions dragged on for almost a year. Although Molly's mom accepted her wrongdoing pretty quickly, Molly packed her stuff, went to live with her dad, and refused to speak with her mom until her mom had "fixed everything." It took Molly's mom quite some time to secure an equity line of credit from a bank that would willingly agree to loan her the money to pay back the company.

*Note to parents:* The facts of each case and home state laws make or break outcomes. One-size outcomes for all cases in all fifty states do not exist.

# CHAPTER 4

*Babies, Commercials, and
Other Special Considerations*

I'm not just saying this. Your baby is *gorgeous*! Have you thought about putting her in commercials?" And so it begins.

The time a parent or parents must put into a pursuit such as getting a child into a commercial is significant, but the monetary rewards, if any, can be slight. For example, print commercial appearances might fetch only a few hundred dollars (depending on the advertiser). A photograph of a "really happy" fourteen-month-old baby sitting atop a pile of diapers might be a perfect image, if chosen, for the sale of a particular diaper brand. However, the photo could be a one-and-done deal. Television commercials, comparatively, generally pay more and include residual royalties paid as long as the commercial runs. If that same baby from the photograph were to be followed by a digital video recorder while doing what babies do—crawling, gurgling, and even "speaking baby"—the diaper manufacturer could traditionally license those recorded action and audio segments for television advertising. With the advent of the Internet and digital handheld devices, moving images can now be found all over to sell a multitude of brands, so demand for talent continues.

*Note to parents:* Read releases and confirmations carefully and ask for experienced assistance before signing them! And if you are seriously contemplating commercial work for your baby, taking inexpensive prints yourself can help keep images current without breaking the bank. As you know, a baby's appearance constantly changes.

The audition process is called a "go-see." Understand that not only is traveling to a go-see unpaid, but the audition is also unpaid. If you are a personal trainer by trade, for example, and receive roughly forty dollars net for each one-hour training session, you likely will not recoup your money. In addition, a personal trainer may have built-in child care at his or her place of employment, but siblings cannot tag along at the audition or commercial work site. Producers are strict about this because the commercial set is their work site, so only one parent to one child is allowed. So along with giving up your regular pay as a personal trainer, you may need to pay additional costs to have your other children looked after. Remember, this is business, not play.

## *Baby's Demeanor and the Fun Factor*

No matter how adorable your baby may be, he or she must also be engaged, happy, and compliant. If your baby is not a good traveler, won't interact with strangers, fusses in public, and is otherwise a chronic whiner, consider a different outlet for fun. If your baby does not tend to follow instructions the first time around, requires ongoing patience with routine matters, and does not appear natural, jolly, and easygoing more days than not, do something else. I know this probably seems like old-fashioned common sense, but after working with people from all walks of life for some years now, I don't think common sense is nearly as common as you might think.

## *Your Demeanor*

Will you mind strangers holding your baby? If the answer is "Yes" or "Maybe," that should tell you that you may likely have a problem because strangers will be holding and working with your baby a lot. It's their job.

## Union Protection

If baby is cast for an on-screen production, the Screen Actors Guild–American Federation of Television and Radio Artists (SAG-AFTRA) will provide protection as long as it's a union production. If you are unsure, ask. There is no union protection, however, for print models, whether babies or adults. Consequently, a strong and reputable agency that can guide parents on fair industry rates is worth its weight in gold.

## State Laws Determine Conditions on Set

State laws and regulations determine who, if anyone, is required to be on set with children at any given time. California requires studio teachers (who are also licensed as welfare workers) to be on set 24-7. For babies under six months, a studio nurse also is required (also see Chapter 5, "Education," and Chapter 6, "Sight, Sound, and Should a Parent Get Paid?"). Remember that there are forty-nine other states, including New York, which is a commercial powerhouse. Some states offer certain protections by law, while others do not.

# A Trade Practice Cleanup by
# Mr. and Mrs. Petersen and the Nurses

Paul Petersen and his wife, Rana Platz-Petersen, RN, formerly the president / business representative for Local 767 of Studio First Aid, part of the industry's union,[27] were involved in successfully advocating for change with respect to using multiple birth babies (e.g., twins and triplets) on production sets. According to Petersen, babies were working lots of odd hours beyond the legal boundary of a two-hour window in the morning and a two-hour window in the afternoon, with a half hour added on for lunch.[28] The rationale behind the legal boundary was that babies need their rest and nap times in addition to a sanitary and safe working environment.

According to Petersen's account, he and his wife Rana worked with the on-set nurses to ensure that the rules were followed. The nurses developed baby call requirements that put baby safety first.[29] (It was also Rana's "baby nurses" that first reported problems with producers using ever-younger premature babies on set—risky to the eyes, lungs, and immune

---

27   Local 767 of Studio First Aid merged with Local 80 of the International Alliance of Theatrical Stage Employees (IATSE).

28   Paul Petersen, "Babies in the Industry," A Minor Consideration, n.d., www.minorcon.org//babiesinindustry.html.

29   Ibid.

system, which aren't ready for the exposure.[30] That practice was eventually plugged by serious legislation in 1998 that mandates compliance and steep fines and/or jail for lawbreakers.[31]) Petersen then followed through by telling producers, "Follow the rules or I will file legal action to rescind your Certificate of Eligibility to Employ Minors."[32] Their interventions worked. Petersen and Platz-Petersen successfully maintained that a baby on set means a baby at work. Twins and triplets should have separate call times. Each baby is assigned an adult in cases where there isn't a second adult guardian.

This emergent history illustrates the importance of all parents and guardians knowing the law and associated regulations in order to protect their child. Knowing the California legal standard should be helpful even if you aren't living in California—it offers a perspective on what works in an entertainment mecca. Knowing the legal standard in New York—also an entertainment mecca—is equally important. Boundaries and the word *no*, especially when it is expressed in an affable, low-key way, may be effective when there is too much emphasis, by an otherwise professional and well-meaning production crew, on cutting costs and red tape at the expense of the kids.

..............................................................................

30    Ibid. and personal e-mail from Paul Petersen, January 31, 2014.

31    See Cal. Lab. Code §1308.8.

32    Petersen, "Babies in the Industry."

This all said, I share with you the opinion of Toni Casala, a child labor specialist in Los Angeles, founder of Children in Film. Inc., and joint venture holder of the New York Studio Teachers' Association. "Sadly, parents have not proven to be the best advocates for their kids. They are too intimidated, especially when starting out. Parents are too scared their kids will lose jobs, and producers sometimes prey on these fears."[33]

## State Rules and Safeguards by Producers, Unions, and Parents

I urge everybody associated with a production, including the family of any child performer and the community at large, to adopt, if they haven't already, a zero tolerance policy for work or production environments that place babies and kids physically or psychologically at risk. (Ensure coverage of work-related insurances paid by the employer/producer, such as workers' compensation, liability, and other work-specific insurances.) This is a no-brainer for professional, competent, and talented producers, studio teachers, as well as many parents or guardians and unions. With producers working under the pressure of being in production, stepping up everyone's

---

33    Personal interview with Toni Casala, March 25, 2014.

game is essential so that special vigilance and attention are paid to child welfare on nonunion sets or in states that do not have relevant laws or sight and/or sound requirements (see Chapter 6, "Sight, Sound, and Should a Parent Get Paid?"). Responsible producers will want parents and guardians to watch over their children when on set. Done seamlessly and without bluster, parents' roles can help make the producer's job easier, in addition to helping keep children safe.

## A Weighty Issue

The pressure to be thin in front of a camera is a central issue— so much so that the state of New York established a Child Performer Advisory Board to Prevent Eating Disorders in 2007. That board has made recommendations about prevention and treatment that tie parental notification of readily available information to the acquisition of the child performer's work permit. Yet it would be naïve to think that any advisory board could remake an industry.

The not-for-profit Model Alliance was founded to improve working conditions in the US fashion industry.[34] The organization quickly made its presence known. In a related event,

........................................................................

34  See the Model Alliance's website at http://modelalliance.org/mission.

hair-raising and dehumanizing accounts compiled by the Independent Democratic Conference[35] entitled *New York's Modeling Crisis: The Importance of Providing Legal Protections for Child Models* featured accounts from courageous industry veterans who were willing to tell their stories.[36] One young woman recounted how at age fourteen "as her body started to develop, her agency pressured her to lose weight. As a result, during her teenage years, [she] struggled with bulimia, which she has since overcome."[37] The New York legislature responded in June 2013 by adding print and runway models to the list of creative or artistic performers protected by its labor code. Governor Andrew Cuomo signed the bill into law a few months later on October 21, 2013. Now, health-related and other safeguards (education, on-set guardian, money set aside) are extended in New York to an all-inclusive list of young artists who model. Protection extends not only to kids who live in New York but

..................................................................

35  The Independent Democratic Conference, established in 2011, is a political party of the New York Senate. It split from the Democratic Caucus and formed a coalition with the Senate Republican Party. See John Celock, "New York State Senate Slips to Republicans via Coalition with Independent Democrats," *Huffington Post*, December 4, 2012, www.huffingtonpost.com/2012/12/04/new-york -state-senate-coalition_n_2238324.html.

36  Independent Democratic Conference, *New York's Modeling Crisis: The Importance of Providing Legal Protections for Child Models*, June 2013, www.nysenate.gov/files/pdfs/IDC%20Report%20Child%20 Model%20Labor%20Laws%202013.pdf.

37  Ibid., p. 9.

also to those who work there and live someplace else. Model industry veteran Joey Grill of New York, cofounder of Click Model Management, Inc., says, "The modification to the existing child performer law in New York State to include 'child models' is a good thing and was the right thing to do. The bottom line is enforcement. I believe most bigger clients, such as advertising agencies, major catalogues, and department stores, will comply with the rules and regulations regarding models under eighteen years of age."[38]

However, there are some industry professionals who are pretty much against it. In the context of Toni Casala's view that parents are not the best advocates for their children, she says that "the problem with the New York Child Performer regulations, as written, is that there is absolutely no mechanism for oversight or enforcement. It's all based on the honor system." She favors instead providing a California-like studio teacher / welfare worker from day one of the production for minors ages fifteen days to fifteen years.[39] Illustrating differences of culture and perspective between the East Coast and West Coast of the United States, however, certain professionals from the Empire State dismiss the California way by saying with resolute finality, "That ain't gonna happen." How many kids will that affect?

................................................................

38   Personal interview with Joey Grill, April 24, 2014.

39   Casala interview.

As of 2011 (before the child performer law extended to models), 6,000 child performers were permitted to work in New York with almost 500 productions permitted to employ child performers.[40] Those numbers, although presently unavailable from that New York labor office, have undoubtedly grown. The economy, in tandem with simmering—if not downright hot—tax incentives, has noticeably improved.

## Good News

Despite the sobering realities of the modeling industry and the natural flow of divergent opinions that coincide, there is good news. "In commercial print, we use all types," said career talent agent Doris Stinga of FunnyFace Today, Inc. (FFT), a thirty-five-year-old talent agency in New York City that first opened its doors as a character modeling agency. "Almost everyone can work from the womb to the tomb," she said (e.g., children, older women, guys who are seven foot five, women who are 450 pounds, musicians, tattoo artists). "I look for chunky boys with personalities who are confident. It is very exciting," she said, going on to describe them as "winners."[41]

........................................................................

40  See the Child Performers Coalition website at
    www.childperformerscoalition.org.

41  Personal interview with Doris Stinga, January 22, 2010.

When I inquired about the existence of a different industry standard for girls compared to boys, Stinga's FFT colleague Charlie Winfield, a talent agent who works with teen models, spoke earnestly about what most of us know: girls develop faster these days. He emphasized the importance of real-age natural beauty. "We want them to be their age. Be who you are. Be your natural self." He also highlighted the fact that talent must be serious about the business. "This isn't a hobby . . . they have to take acting classes. It isn't just about a certain look. They need to be engaging. They have to know how to speak because it is so competitive . . . to assimilate with every age group."[42] Learning how to communicate with younger people, older folks, and everyone in between enhances a young model's marketability. Winfield knows what he is talking about. He became a child model at the age of six when his parents—on a whim—put him in acting classes. He went on to play the Sesame Street character Grover for a touring show. Winfield stayed in front of the camera until he was twenty-four. Speaking about the value of communication from a first go-see through rate negotiation and payment, FFT colleague and agent Fabiola Osorio stressed preparation and the parents' role. "We make sure at every stage, we apprise the parents."[43]

........................................................................

42   Personal interview with Charlie Winfield, January 22, 2010.

43   Personal interview with Fabiola Osorio, January 22, 2010.

# CHAPTER 5

*Education*

K eeping up grades to ensure eligibility for a work permit should not, in my view, be the prime reason to emphasize the importance of education in a child's life. A solid education will serve a child for a lifetime and is good insurance against an often fleeting career as a young performer. That said, let's face it: the quality of education that a child performer receives might vary greatly, depending on many factors. Attending a traditional school with classmates who can be friends and an abundance of class choices, clubs, activities, field trips, learning support services, counseling, and college and career guidance is a very different experience from being schooled on set. Similarly, home school curriculums vary from one state to another and even from one school district to another, so those offer a yet different experience from being taught in a traditional school or on set.

It is important to acknowledge the value of the learning and enrichment that can come with participating in a commercial production or a series of productions. Parents are uniquely positioned to assess whether their child is up to making the trade-offs. In instances where it is not possible to continue attending a traditional school, some children, particularly as they grow older, may also display good insight with respect to weighing whether the value of the professional experience is worth giving up the traditional learning environment. Ideally, children will gain practical, professional performance experience while also receiving a solid education.

Educating children from varied state school systems layered with regional requirements that measure a child's academic performance makes for a highly technical tapestry. Fold in the requirement that a child must earn solid academic performance to acquire some state work permits, and you have the interesting blend of academic performance and permission to work driving a child's education.[44] Regardless of what state laws say, parents must tend carefully to their child's education. Do not assume that it is someone else's job to protect the quality and integrity of your child's schooling or that balancing what your child gets and what he or she gives up rests on someone else's shoulders. That job belongs to you as a parent. Before scheduling, juggling, and fulfilling commercial demands, make appointments with teachers, principals, and other

---

44 Presuming a working child's good health.

decision makers. Figure out what needs to be done to get your child what he or she needs, then do it!

On Location Education's Alan Simon cautions that "you want to match the right teacher for the child. But understand that if your child is an AP [advanced placement] student, you are not going to necessarily have AP appropriate-level classes when he or she is one of four students and the production company budget pays for one teacher for every ten students. It is beyond you."[45] What may not be beyond the parent's control, however, is to push for a change in an assigned studio teacher. Simon also notes that doing homework in addition to working as a professional and attending on-location classes can be quite difficult. To illustrate the difficulties that can arise, he relayed one parent's complaint that they "live in Cherry Hill, New Jersey, a four-hour round-trip commute to and from the stage. With three hours per day required for teaching time . . . homework is not possible."

Simon is similarly knowledgeable about the production company's perspective and believes that the producer can be uniquely vested in the quality of the child's education. "If, for example, producers know they are going to have sixteen kids on set from ages seven to sixteen, the company could

.....................................................................

45   A. Simon interview.

appropriate three teachers as opposed to two." He underscored that the greater the lead time, the easier it is for the producer to achieve quality. He cited theatre productions that tour the United States and Broadway shows, in particular, as offering the maximum amount of time for education planning because itineraries include start dates, and commitment dates are known in advance. Film, television, and the recording industries, he noted, don't routinely have that same expansive window to offer producers before production begins.

The recent New York State amendment that offers protection for print and runway models now offers the same required and regulated education for minors working as print and runway models as it offers to other child performers. The timing of the legislature's green light coincided with the *New York's Modeling Crisis* study[46] (see Chapter 4, "Babies, Commercials, and Other Special Considerations"). That published report described staff at agencies encouraging children to miss school or drop out altogether. One agency expected a young model to work late into the night until her parents intervened, and she stopped modeling until after graduating from high school. Although that revelation and others may shock some, I cannot imagine such a reaction would be shared by every industry insider knowledgeable

........................................................

46   Independent Democratic Conference, *New York's Modeling Crisis.*

about the competitive modeling industry. Moreover, there are many reasons some parents drop off their fifteen-year-old daughter in New York City and entrust her career to a model management company. Quoting one source (on the condition of anonymity), "Sometimes it's a stage mother syndrome, in which the parent lives their own dream vicariously through the child's career. Sometimes it's as basic as the parent's desire to help their child fulfill their own dream. They come to New York because that is where the center of modeling in America is. The families rarely have enough money to relocate, and on balance it is the best way to accomplish being in New York City."

## *Education's Importance*[47]

- Jodie Foster, at seventeen, was asked by the late Roger Ebert what she wanted to see happen in the next five years. Foster said, "School, first and foremost. I don't think I'll take any film classes. Yale has a wonderful drama school, and I want to study that."[48] She grad-

...............................................................

47   See Luchina Fisher, "Emma Watson Left Brown but Other Child Stars Become College Grads," *ABC News*, June 9, 2011, http:// abcnews.go.com/Entertainment/emma-watson-leaves-brown-child-stars-college-grads/story?id=13792246#.Ud61axzG9M5.

48   Roger Ebert, "Jodie Foster Goes to College," April 13, 1980, www .jodiefosterfan.com/press/interviews/jodie-foster-goes-to-college.

uated magna cum laude from Yale University with a bachelor's degree in literature. Her illustrious career has earned her two Academy Awards, three BAFTA Awards, two Golden Globe Awards, a Screen Actors Guild Award, two People's Choice Awards, and two Emmy nominations.[49]

- Brooke Shields graduated from Princeton University with honors. She focused on romance languages.[50] When she spoke on Class Day 2011, she told the students, "Without the four years of learning and growth that culminated in my degree, I would have never survived my industry, a business that predicates itself on eating its young."[51] She added, "I would have become a cliché. I would never have been able to adapt and to re-invent: from movies to television, to stage, to author, to mom."[52]

.................................................................

49   See Gus Lubin, "The 30 Most Famous Yale Students of All Time," *Business Insider*, June 11, 2010, www.businessinsider.com/30-most-famous-yale-2010-5#jodie-foster-ba-1985-in-literature-magna-cum-laude-25.

50   See Dina Spector and Vivian Giang, "The 25 Most Famous Princeton Students of All Time," *Business Insider*, December 1, 2011, www.businessinsider.com/famous-princeton-students-2011-11.

51   Fisher, "Emma Watson Left Brown."

52   Ibid.

- Natalie Portman graduated from Harvard University with a bachelor's degree in psychology. Fox News quoted her as saying, "I don't care if [college] ruins my career . . . I'd rather be smart than a movie star."[53]

- Jerry O'Connell, the eleven-year-old in the film *Stand by Me*, graduated from New York University where he studied screen writing.[54]

- Claire Danes returned to acting after two years at Yale University, explaining to the *Washington Post*, "I'm sure I missed something but I learned how to think critically and read and write. I felt basically fulfilled."[55]

- Emma Watson, the *Harry Potter* star who debuted on screen at age eleven, explained her decision to leave Brown University for another school after eighteen months by saying, "I wanted to pretend I wasn't as famous as I was. I was trying to seek out normality, but I kind of have to accept who I am, the position I'm in

......................................................................

53   Ibid. Also see "Cerebral Celebs Give Up Screen for Studies," Fox News, May 23, 2002, www.foxnews.com/story/2002/05/23/cerebral-celebs-give-up-screen-for-studies.html.

54   Fisher, "Emma Watson Left Brown."

55   Ibid. Also see Valerie Strauss, "Talking Out of School: Claire Danes on College, Getting Tutored on TV and Her So-Called Life," *Washington Post*, December 31, 2009, http://voices.washingtonpost.com/answer-sheet/talking-out-of-school/talking-out-of-school-how-clai.html.

and what happened."[56] In fact, she returned to Brown University, earning a bachelor of arts in English literature in May 2014.[57]

Now consider these other stars:

- Haley Joel Osment graduated from the Tisch School of the Arts at New York University in 2010.[58] He earned an Academy Award nomination within six years of being discovered for his role in *The Sixth Sense*.[59] The actor credited his parents for making a "tremendous effort to have a home life, education, and community that preserved the privacy and freedom kids need."[60]

- Before he became a Grammy winner, John Legend graduated from the University of Pennsylvania where

---

56   Fisher, "Emma Watson Left Brown."

57   See Lauren Duca, "Emma Watson Set to Graduate from Brown University with English Literature Degree," *Huffington Post,* May 25, 2014, www.huffingtonpost.com/2014/05/25/emma-watson-brown_n_5389191.html.

58   Sarah Bernard, "Celebs Who Went Back to College After Becoming Famous," *Babble*, 2014, www.babble.com/entertainment/celebs-who-went-back-to-college-after-becoming-famous.

59   Simon Parkin, "Haley Joel Osment Returns," *New Yorker*, October 29, 2014, www.newyorker.com/culture/culture-desk/haley-joel-osment.

60   Nate Jones, "Life After *The Sixth Sense*: Haley Joel Osment Still in Awe of Bruce Willis's 'Radiant Manliness,'" *People Magazine,* January 21, 2014, www.people.com/people/article/0,,20777069,00.html.

he majored in English with an emphasis on African American literature.[61] But long before receiving his singer-songwriter accolades, this star's grandmother taught her child-prodigy grandson how to play the piano, and during his formative years he sang in the church choir.[62]

· Fred Savage graduated from Stanford University with a bachelor of arts in English in 1999.[63] He was cast alongside Danica McKellar in *The Wonder Years*. When the show ended, he went back to high school to finish his senior year, acted in the school musical, and even played on the football team.[64] "It was almost like we had this fantastic extracurricular activity," Savage was quoted as saying. "All of us had these really full lives

61   Sam Brodey, "19 Celebrities Who Graduated from Really Good Colleges," *Arts.Mic*, March 28, 2014, http://mic.com/articles/86351/19-celebrities-who-graduated-from-really-good-colleges.

62   See "John Legend Biography," Bio., www.biography.com/people/john-legend-201302.

63   See Leah Goldman and Vivian Gang, "The 25 Most Famous Stanford Students of All Time, *Business Insider*, June 28, 2011, www.businessinsider.com/famous-stanford-students-2011-6#fred-savage-earned-his-ba-in-1999-24.

64   Mike Ayers, "Fred Savage's New Wonder Years," *GQ*, May 2, 2012, www.gq.com/entertainment/movies-and-tv/201205/fred-savage-wonder-years-director-always-sunny-philadelphia-party-down.

waiting for us with friends and a life outside the entertainment world."[65]

- Danica McKellar graduated summa cum laude from the University of California, Los Angeles (UCLA), with a bachelor's degree in mathematics, and even proved a new math theorem, the Chayes-McKellar-Winn theorem, with a fellow student under the guidance of their professor.[66] An accomplished writer, McKellar has authored three *New York Times* bestselling books and was cast in *Dancing with the Stars* in 2014.[67]

- Greg Graffin, the prolific musician of punk band Bad Religion fame, formed the band in his teens with three school friends. He earned two undergraduate degrees from UCLA, one in biology and the other in geology.[68] He later earned a PhD in zoology from Cornell, and he

........................................................

65  Reed Tucker, "Catching Up with Fred Savage and Danica McKellar of *The Wonder Years*," *New York Post*, October 23, 2014, http://nypost.com/2014/10/23/catching-up-with-fred-savage-and-danica-mckellar-of-the-wonder-years.

66  See "Danica McKellar '98: Recent Graduate Achievement Award," *UCLA Alumni*, n.d., http://alumni.ucla.edu/share/ucla-awards/bio/danica-mckellar.aspx.

67  See www.danicamckellar.com/about/ and www.danicamckellar.com/blog/Events-Appearances/Dancing+with+the+Stars.

68  See "Greg Graffin Biography," Bio., n.d., www.biography.com/people/greg-graffin-21008709.

regularly teaches geology classes at UCLA. Graffin is coauthor of two books on science and religion.[69]

- Brian May is a founding member of Queen; a world-renowned guitarist, songwriter, producer, and performer; and has a doctorate in astrophysics from Imperial College London. May began playing guitar at age seven and soon formed his first band at school.[70] He built a custom-made guitar, the "Red Special," as a teenager.[71] He achieved his doctorate after a thirty-year break in his education.[72]

- Christy Turlington Burns left modeling to study at New York University full-time. She graduated cum laude and holds a bachelor's degree in comparative religion and Eastern philosophy. She is currently pursuing a master's degree at Columbia University's Mailman School of Public Health.[73]

.......................................................................

69    "Doctors of Rock: 10 Musicians with PhDs," TheBestColleges.org, November 12, 2010, www.thebestcolleges.org/doctors-of-rock-10-musicians-with-phds.

70    "Brian May Biography," Famous People, n.d., www.thefamouspeople .com/profiles/brian-may-3689.php.

71    See "Brian May Biography," Bio.

72    "Brian May Biography," Bio., n.d., www.thebiographychannel.co.uk/ biographies/brian-may.html.

73    Molly Knight Raskin, "Model Citizen: Christy Turlington Burns," *Capitol File*, n.d., http://capitolfile-magazine.com/personalities/ articles/model-citizen-2.

And then there's James Franco. His story is included here as a means for comparison because his career blended with his ongoing academic pursuits beyond childhood.

- James Franco left UCLA after his first year to pursue acting, but later he decided that "acting didn't feed his soul."[74] At age twenty-eight, he returned to UCLA "and found classes so magically satisfying—so safe and pure compared with the world of acting—that he threw himself back into his education with crazy abandon . . . [then] proceeded to take 62 credits a quarter, roughly three times the normal limit. . . . He graduated in two years with a degree in English and a GPA over 3.5."[75] He continued acting while enrolled. He has a master's degree in fine arts from Columbia University, and a PhD in English from Yale University.[76]

........................................................................

74  Amy Raphael, "Acting Clever," *Guardian*, January 23, 2009, www .theguardian.com/film/2009/jan/24/james-franco-interview-milk.

75  "The James Franco Project," *New York Magazine*, n.d., http://nymag .com/movies/profiles/67284/index1.html.

76  See Amy Raphael and Megan Bedard, "Fifteen Celebrities with Degrees That Will Surprise You," *Guardian*, August 4, 2012, www .takepart.com/photos/15-celebrities-surprising-degrees/james-franco.

# The Studio Teacher and California Law

Studio teachers are required to educate minors in California every day that a production contracts for a child performer, starting on day one. They are retained by the production company and are also considered welfare workers. In addition to teaching, the studio teacher has the responsibility of caring and attending to the health, safety, and morals of minors under age sixteen while the minors are engaged or employed in any activity pertaining to the entertainment industry. Factors the studio teachers must consider include working conditions; physical surroundings; signs of the minor's mental and physical fatigue; and the demands placed upon the minor in relation to the minor's age, agility, strength, and stamina. The studio teacher may refuse to allow the minor on a set or location and may remove the minor from a set or location if, in his or her judgment, conditions present a danger to the health, safety, or morals of the minor. The studio teacher's action may be immediately appealed to the labor commissioner, who may affirm or countermand—that is, cancel—the action.[77]

A studio teacher's role is unusual—and crucial—for the production to be compliant with the law. Daily requirements

---

77   Cal. Code Regs. tit. 8, § 11755.3 (2015).

for the number of hours set aside for a child to learn together with the number of hours permitted on set, and nuanced by rest periods, can best be fulfilled with a teacher's toolbox that contains insight into how productions work, a stopwatch, and one affable but effective personality.

However, at the risk of offending hardworking and talented studio teachers who have unflappable integrity and an ethical, cement-based compass that points squarely in the direction of the kids' best interests and needs, consider the following points: When we were young students, once upon a time, we understood that all teachers were not the same. They came in all shapes and sizes, and some were—to put it bluntly—smarter and more talented than others. Some wore happy faces, and others never owned or even attempted to borrow one. As we grew older, we began to realize that there were some pretty good reasons for what we saw and experienced. For example, school budgets that stretch and require an otherwise superbly talented and even-tempered teacher to educate a class of thirty-five students would likely dash many a spirit. Many school systems are laden with tenured teachers who have long since lost their joy for teaching but continue to hang on for benefits such as health insurance and pension funds. As a final example, consider that neighborhoods are often stocked with children who come from households where the parent(s) or other family members and caretakers work multiple jobs and are not home after school or even in the early evening hours to oversee homework time.

Now let's consider studio teachers, who may earn less than traditional educators, be required to travel with the production, and work in less than ideal conditions. Can that studio teacher, on an ongoing basis, fulfill his or her obligation to *every* minor when dependent upon the production company for his or her livelihood? Because of the possibility of reprisal, can that same teacher literally afford to buck the system? Is there an all too human temptation to be more accepting of certain conditions on set or on location that carry greater risk or less benefit for the kids?

Scott Plimpton, a California studio teacher and welfare worker with more than ten years of experience, describes the situation as follows:

Studio teachers play a vital role on set. We are the only production members whose sole job responsibility is to look after the children. Besides their welfare, we are responsible for their education and enforcing applicable labor laws. Primarily, these laws mandate how long a child can be on set or in school, and guarantee minimum rest and meal breaks. The rules vary depending on the age of the minor and whether school is in session and can be affected by many other factors. This is important enough that we are legally required to be hired when minors are working. When on a job, I like to think that studio teachers have the legal authority, parents have the moral authority, and production has the logistical authority when it comes to caring for the kids. Working together as a team, we can create a positive and productive experience for everyone involved.

Not very many children get the opportunity to work professionally in the entertainment industry. Of those who do, even fewer go on to become adult actors. Most of the kids I have worked with could easily qualify for the gifted and talented programs at their regular schools. All of them need, and deserve, the best education possible. A studio teacher should feel like a parent's ally on set and be a resource for any questions they might have. If a parent doesn't feel supported, they should approach the teacher with their concerns. Nobody should settle for substandard care of their children.[78]

---

78  Personal interview with Scott Plimpton, September 12, 2013.

If and when circumstances arise that can accommodate a parent or guardian's selection of a studio teacher instead of a producer/employer, seize the opportunity. Whatever your sensibilities on this topic, it rightly frames the foundation for requiring a parent or guardian to be within sight and/or sound of the young performer and to speak up. If you are looking to get into the weeds on specific educational requirements, start with Chapter 14, "Tables and Resources."

# CHAPTER 6

*Sight, Sound, and*
*Should a Parent Get Paid?*

Even if they wanted to, could all parents of all talented children working in all fifty US states just drop their kids off to work in show biz? Can production companies beholden to union rules and state laws just shoo parents away? The short answer to both questions is "No."

- If a minor is cast in a Screen Actors Guild production, there exists a parental right and responsibility to be within sight and sound of a child performer.
- If a child is working in a state with sight and/or sound laws or other laws that address work and labor requirements, those laws govern the work conditions.

Okay, you say. This seems like a simple enough concept, and one rooted in a safety-first protective sleeve. However, the process isn't so simple. Why? Because union rules and state laws and regulations aren't all the same. Those differences affect how productions work. It's a lot of information for parents to digest and apply . . . and that, understandably, takes time.

# SAG-AFTRA

The Screen Actors Guild (SAG), in a historic move, merged with the American Federation of Television and Radio Artists (AFTRA) on March 30, 2012. Currently, the membership roster is approximately 160,000 strong.[79] As of March 31, 2015, nearly 4,200 members are minors.[80] Whether or not an individual state has a sight and/or sound law or other workplace laws for kids, SAG-AFTRA places minimum standards on minor supervision, engagement, and employment. So if an employer is SAG-AFTRA affiliated, this means that the employer has agreed to be bound by SAG-AFTRA's terms and conditions and to do what SAG-AFTRA requires. Of special note, the union emphasizes that the parent or guardian should be fully acquainted with contract provisions to "ensure SAG-AFTRA contracts are fully enforced" in addition to applicable state laws and blocked trust accounts. This underscores the parent or guardian's (ultimate) responsibility to ensure the young performer is treated fairly.[81] Especially for parents new to show business, these responsibilities can be overwhelming.

---

79  See the SAG-AFTRA website at www.sagaftra.org/content/membership.

80  Information provided by SAG-AFTRA, April 7, 2015.

81  *Working for You*, SAG-AFTRA, n.d., http://www.sagaftra.org/workingforyou.

The *Young Performers Handbook* Presented by Screen Actors Guild (*Handbook*, 2010) advises parents to call its contracts department in Los Angeles at (855) SAG-AFTRA ([855] 724-2387) to obtain the applicable contract to become familiar with engagement, employment, and supervision.[82] SAG-AFTRA also informs parents that they may wish to call the local SAG-AFTRA office where their child is working. You can also visit www.sagaftra.org/content/young-performers or www.sagaftra.org/production-center for more information or to obtain actual contracts.

*Note to parents:* Your child's role or participation will determine which specialized SAG-AFTRA contract is applicable. Every SAG-AFTRA contract is not the same. (Since contracts are renegotiated every three years, make sure you have the current one.) Similarly, most Actors' Equity Association (Equity) contracts are negotiated every three to four years. Equity is the labor union that represents more than 50,000 stage actors and stage managers in the United States, thus fostering the art of live theatre.[83] (Other performing arts unions, by the way, include the American Guild of Variety Artists and the American

82    Screen Actors Guild, *Young Performers Handbook*, SAG-AFTRA Young Performers, 2010, http://youngperformers.sagaftra.org/files/youngperformers/YPH_FNL3.pdf.

83    "About Equity," Actors' Equity Association, n.d., www.actorsequity.org/AboutEquity/aboutequityhome.asp.

Guild of Musical Artists. These four unions make up the 4As: Associated Actors and Artistes of America.) Do not cut corners when it comes to contracts—union and otherwise. Unless you have a keen legal mind and proven and relevant expertise with contract legalese in the particular industry in which your son or daughter is working—enough so that you really understand what the contract says and understand its legal ramifications and the law—find someone you trust for their professional experience and legal understanding and ask them to read the contract and explain it to you. Do not be intimidated by print. Union standards are minimum standards. That means that, with leverage, some terms may be negotiated more favorably. Contract terms, in other words, may be revised and added to, depending on the contract type.

To give you a sense of some of the union terms, the following provisions appear in the 2005 SAG Motion Picture and Television Contract for Producers, which is referenced online as the "SAG/2005 Theatrical Agreement (Motion Picture & TV)":

> A parent or guardian must be present at all times while a minor is working, and shall have the right, subject to filming requirements, to be within sight and sound of the minor (with exceptions). When a parent is working at the minor's place of employment but not at the scene of employment, either the other parent or a guardian

must be present with the minor. A guardian . . . must be at least 18 years of age, have the written permission of the minor's parent(s) to act as a guardian, and show sufficient maturity to be approved by Producer. Presence of the teacher does not relieve parents . . . of the responsibility of caring for their own children.[84]

Also, and in accordance with the SAG-AFTRA website, which consistently emphasizes workplace safety:

SAG-AFTRA reps are "on set" to protect all members, but especially working children. It is their job to ensure that all SAG-AFTRA rules, including work hours and safety rules, are being followed.

When children are on set, your SAG-AFTRA rep is keeping an eye out for the following:

1. Are children being asked to work overtime or beyond the permitted work hours?

2. Are children getting adequate meals and rest periods?

3. Are they being tutored in a safe and effective manner?

4. Have they been asked to do hazardous work?

5. Are parents permitted to be within sight and sound of the child at all times?

..........................................................

84 *General Provisions*, SAG-AFTRA, n.d., www.sagaftra.org/files/sag/2005theatricalagreement.pdf. See p. 111.

6. Have the children been provided an appropriate dressing room area?

So when a SAG-AFTRA rep says hello to you and asks you how things are going, don't hesitate to speak up. They cannot be in all places at all times and count on the help of the child's primary guardian to inform them of any problems or concerns. Our representatives are on set to help you, so don't hesitate to take advantage of their expertise and authority. If you need to get in touch with a SAG-AFTRA field representative, please call the union at (855) SAG-AFTRA. SAG-AFTRA field representatives are available 24 hours a day.[85]

Placing SAG-AFTRA rules into perspective, according to the *Handbook*, minors who work in Motion Picture and Television (under a Theatrical Contract) apply to young people under age eighteen (18).[86] The other major agreements such as Theatrical/TV, Network Code, Corporate Educational, and Sound Recordings also define a minor as under age eighteen (18). However, minors who work in commercials apply to

...................................................................

85  "For Parents," SAG-AFTRA, n.d., www.sagaftra.org/content/for-parents.

86  Unless a young performer (a) has satisfied the compulsory education laws of the state governing his/her employment, (b) is married, (c) is a member of the armed forces, or (d) is legally emancipated.

young people fifteen (15) and under.[87] This means that certain union requirements may offer protection longer than some state laws that offer protection to kids for a shorter time period (e.g., until the age of sixteen) and enhanced protection—for example, "sight *and* sound" (union) versus "sight *or* sound" (state). See below for how the laws in California and New York read.

By the way, not all minors need to join the union to work in a SAG-AFTRA production. These types of provisions are known as *union security*. If you stop to think about it, the term makes sense. Minimum rates and requirements exist to protect union members depending on the production and their role. Consequently, the level of protection mandated by the union depends on what its associated contract says. So, for example, minors under age four who are cast in a principal role and minors under age fourteen who are cast as a background performer under a Theatrical Contract need not join the union. Also, minors under age four who are cast in either a principal or background role under a Commercial or Industrial Contract need not join the union.

The preceding may feel overly "legal" to you, but stick with me. It's like riding a bicycle: once you get it, you won't forget it.

........................................................................

87    Screen Actors Guild, *Handbook*, p. 30.

Now let's take a look at California and New York laws.

California: "A parent or guardian of a minor under sixteen (16) . . . must be present with, and accompany, such minor on the set or location and be within sight or sound at all times."[88]

New York: The Empire State requires that a "responsible person" (over eighteen years old) be assigned to every child performer under age sixteen. New regulations by the New York State Department of Labor went into effect on April 1, 2013.[89] The duties of the responsible person include monitoring the child's safety and well-being throughout the workday and accompanying the child throughout the workday. A parent or guardian can either serve or pick someone else to serve as the responsible person. If a parent or guardian drops the ball and doesn't do this, the child's employer must step in and designate another adult. That person can be responsible for more than one child. Live theatre or other live performances (e.g., Broadway) trigger additional regulations "where it is physically impracticable for the employer to permit a responsible person designated by the parent or guardian to accompany a child under 16."[90] Then the employer may either employ a

88   See Cal. Code Regs. tit. 8 §11757 (2015).

89   See NY CLS Labor §154-a, 12 NYCRR §186-1–§186-10-1 (2013).

90   *Part 186: Child Performers*, New York State Department of Labor, www.labor.ny.gov/legal/laws/pdf/child_performer/text-of-the-rule.pdf.

responsible person or provide the responsible person designated by the parent or guardian with facilities to observe and hear the child through electronic or other appropriate means, or both. In instances where the employer elects to employ a responsible person, the employer must notify the parent or guardian in writing of the name of the responsible person, who may be responsible for more than one child, and shall, at the employer's election, either (a) obtain the written agreement of the parent or guardian, which shall not be unreasonably withheld or delayed; or (b) provide the parent or guardian with an opportunity to object to the responsible person and provide a mechanism to timely address any reasonable objections in the best interest of the child.[91]

Prior to April 1, 2013, much work and spirited debate were directed at the New York State Department of Labor in order to build the new regulations.[92] The Child Performers Coalition (www.childperformerscoalition.org) was founded to educate and unite parents who felt excluded from early-stage participation, and it played a pivotal role along with other groups and

91    See NY CLS Labor §154-a, 12 NYCRR §186-1–§186-10-1 (2013), at Subpart 186-4.6(a)–(d)(1)(2).

92    NY CLS Labor §154-a mandates the labor commissioner to "promulgate such regulations determining the hours and conditions of work necessary to safeguard the health, education, morals, and general welfare of child performers."

individuals. Critical of proposed rules that appeared to allow employers the discretion to deny a child over the age of five sight and sound access to his or her parent and instead appoint a responsible person to monitor the child throughout the workday, the coalition branded the potential sight and sound provision as "the single most dangerous provision in the proposed rule."[93] Child Performers Coalition founder Kelly Crisp, a former felony prosecutor, rallied member parents. She asserted the coalition's belief that "with very few exceptions, the child's parent is the best advocate for the interests of the child."[94] Genuine fear of pedophiles' access to kids screamed for attention. The coalition also made the point that children who don't work under union umbrellas (unions insist on a parent's sight and sound access) and who work on nonunion sets face greater vulnerability and risk, noting the likelihood that such children have less work experience and less understanding of the dangers inherent in working on set.[95] Nonunion sets are often less professional and less controlled, with corners being routinely cut, which leaves nonunion actors even more

.......................................................................

93   Child Performers Coalition segment referencing Child Performers Coalition Final Position Statement to the New York State Department of Labor, approved by Kelly Crisp on March 19, 2015.

94   Ibid.

95   Ibid.

vulnerable than their union counterparts and in need of more protection, not less.[96]

*Special note:* In 2011, a notable former child actor courageously spoke out about his experiences and feelings about pedophilia in the entertainment industry in an ABC *Nightline* interview. "Former child star Corey Feldman said in a televised interview that 'the No. 1 problem in Hollywood was and is and always will be pedophilia.'"[97] The risk to kids, in his view, was and remains all too real.

Now consider worry from parents and place it next to an unscripted production without either union or sight or sound protection. Particular care must be taken to read any participant agreement. This is the contract that producers require parents and their "participating child(ren)" to sign. Sometimes, the language can be "over the top crazy," for example, giving a producer free rein to make medical decisions for a child or consenting to oversee and supervise a child's physical, emotional, and mental well-being without any parental supervision. (I don't want to spoil the next chapter, so I'll stop here.)

........................................................................

96    Ibid.

97    Daniel Tovrov, "Corey Feldman: Pedophilia Is 'Hollywood's Big Secret,'" *International Business Times,* August 12, 2011, www.ibtimes.com/corey-feldman-pedophilia-hollywoods-big-secret-832581.

Other concerns were raised—not only from parents and other child advocates but also by unions, producers, studios, and other industries and interest groups in areas such as education. Treating unscripted shows ("reality TV") as employment was a mighty large fly in the ointment, too. Sparring occurred openly and in meetings with the New York State Department of Labor. A polarization of opinions characterized the public process, with parents and sometimes others apparently feeling like relatives locked out of their own home for Thanksgiving dinner. After an extended deadline and a much-anticipated ruling, the process first ended temporarily in a dramatic fizzle. Then the process of integrating the public's contributions, professional views, and the Department of Labor's assessments was started up again. This time, after yet another public comment period that ended on or about October 22, 2012, the New York State Department of Labor ruled decisively, launching its new and revised regulations for child performers on April 1, 2013, that included print and runway models and reality show participants on its existing list of young performers. Seventy-six people submitted written comments, and twenty-six people spoke at the hearings, fourteen of whom also submitted written comments, for a total of eighty-eight people formally submitting comments.[98] In the end, democracy prevailed. The Department of Labor team managed to effectively regulate an evolution governing the employment and participation of children over the preceding decade through the public hearing process.

*Note to parents:* If a child lives and/or works in another state, that state may or may not have a sight and/or sound rule or regulation. Even if it does not have a formal rule or regulation, the state may, nonetheless, have labor laws and work permit requirements that protect children. And don't forget: if your child is working for a SAG-AFTRA production, your child's employer must comply with (a) the local child labor laws and regulations (e.g., work permitting) in any jurisdiction where your child is working and (b) SAG-AFTRA provisions. If a local law or regulation is more restrictive than the union's provision, the employer must adjust to and comply with the local law. If the local law or regulation is either less restrictive or does not exist, then the employer must comply with the union's provision. Here's a good example: whether or not a child is a California resident, a sight and sound requirement controls in a state where there is no law or regulation.

..............................................................

98  *Summary of Revised Proposed Rule Making,* New York State Department of Labor, n.d., www.labor.state.ny.us/legal/laws/pdf/child_performer/summary-of-text.pdf.

Let's not forget about the provisions made for *juvenile actors*, the term that Equity uses for young stage performers. An excerpt of those rules and how to contact that union can be found in Chapter 14, "Tables and Resources."

## What Ifs

Parents can defer the responsibility of sight and/or sound to a competent and capable grown-up, according to the New York model, as long as the designee meets reasonable criteria rooted in the child's best interest, provided that

- both the parent or guardian and the company agree on the person or
- the parent makes the selection in the first place.

If the selection isn't working out in light of the director/producer's consideration of straightforward criteria—such as timely arrival, professional performance, and the meeting of educational requirements—a parent would, after being notified, be required to take over. Period.

## Time and Money

Peeling back the onion layers, the underlying issues include the following:

- The time involved
- The opportunity cost for a parent who might otherwise be employed
- Whether the parent or parents can really afford to pursue these opportunities on behalf of their child

Parents who work outside the home must decide whether they are able to invest the time required to take their child to auditions, practices, and productions and if this pursuit is financially practical or even possible for them. Parents considering the commercial placement of their child before an audience must do the math on the affordability of this mandatory right or requirement well in advance. (See Chapter 1, "Considerations for Parents.")

For a print commercial that pays $200, could parents with private practices in law or medicine easily justify taking a lot of time off work to pursue a career for their son or daughter? Using the good ol' cost-benefit analysis for the possibility of a job that pays $200 to the child, will the lawyer mom or dad consistently forgo a day of billable time? If the lawyer's hourly rate is $400 and he or she calculates that getting the child a job involves no less than a ten-hour commitment (after tallying the time for driving, auditioning [go-sees], telephone calls with either a talent agent or other agency, and the actual production), approximately $4,000 of billable time is at stake for a $200 fee. This calculation does not even include the difficulties that can result when a lawyer goes missing in action for a day or two here and there, which can affect not only his or her partnership or company but also his or her clients. Could a medical doctor take the necessary amount of time away from his or her practice, and at what cost and price to the patients and the practice? Of course, some lawyers and doctors can make this work because they have the flexibility to do so. The flip side of that argument could incite righteous indignation from detractors who say that parents working as doctors or private practice lawyers generally earn more and, therefore, have the means to afford the time off. The doctors or lawyers will sometimes reply, "Money maybe, time no."

Then again, many parents who work seriously, responsibly, and in time-intensive positions but who aren't lawyers or doctors may earn healthy incomes. Could those parents take time off, and if so, how easily? Could parents who work for a thirty-five-dollar hourly wage, for instance, justify and afford time away from work? What if those same people earn a salary, and to earn that salary they are required to be at their office from 8:00 a.m. to 5:00 p.m. or even later?

To compensate for the financial losses that are commonly triggered when a young performer works regularly, some parents elect to become their son's or daughter's manager. According to Paul Petersen, "They become the 'momager' or 'popager' at 15 percent of their child's gross compensation."[99]

Underscoring Petersen's point, critics lament that some petitioning parents are not qualified to serve as managers because they don't have the background, training, education or experience to do it, while others lack job skills that would make them marketable and employable in other fields.

In instances where a parent doesn't have the industry experience to guide, counsel, and advise his or her child in all aspects of the entertainment industry (a bedrock obligation of personal managers), a solution that might benefit the child would be for the parent to be paid for sight and/or sound service. (Parents, in some instances, are already using the child's income to pay others for services related to the child's employment.) More about this later. Now let's view this as providing a solution that might serve as an incentive.

So should a parent get paid?

..........................................................................

99   Petersen interview.

Let's start from the beginning. Most parents would not have the sight and/or sound rule any different than it is. They want to be with their kids in order to ensure their safety and well-being. We saw an example of this when parents united against the possibility of uprooting parental access in New York.

- By parents supervising their child, the child's risk of being physically or emotionally injured while working decreases.
- Simultaneously, the risks of the production company employing the child go down.
- In addition, union requirements are satisfied.

Based on the preceding considerations, the following benefits occur when sight and/or sound rules are in place:

- Risks to the child are minimized.
- Parental concerns are minimized, providing parents with a sense of control and a source of comfort.
- Liability to the production company is minimized.
- All parties are union compliant.

But not everyone derives a benefit. Remember that sight and/or sound protection is not automatic. Recall that children guaranteed the protection include those of particular ages who work for specific union productions or receive coverage according to a state law or regulation offering a sight and/or sound rule or other similar requirement.

To determine if it makes sense for a parent to get paid, consider whether a parental benefit should be factored in. The following questions are relevant:

- Should parents be paid, regardless of whether or not they receive a benefit?
- Should a benefit to the production company or other employer justify parental compensation?
- Assuming that parents receive a benefit, should there be no compensation?

If you don't think parents should be paid, you may feel that parents knew or should have known that their kids would be paid, not them, and that it was their duty to assess whether they could afford to indulge their child's interest in performing on a professional level while also continuing to meet the ordinary support obligations of their child or children in the process. You may also feel that supervising one's child is a form of parenting and support and that meeting those obligations requires the parents to pay and not the other way around. Thinking it through, you may wonder if paying a parent really means that a child, who may be paying for family living expenses (not just his own), will now be required to pay his mother or father, too.

You may feel strongly that parents who already receive management fees should not receive more money.

On the other hand, you may feel that parents should be paid regardless of any benefits they may derive from the experience because parents' time has value, and if not for them, their kids wouldn't be working. (This is undoubtedly the rationale of some parents who have either drawn a salary or a consulting fee from their child's earnings.) You may even wholeheartedly agree with those who don't believe parents should be paid but also recognize that paying a parent an hourly or per diem wage in lieu of a 15 percent parent management fee might mean more money is left for the child.

Realizing that this issue may best be vetted in the court of public opinion, under legislative domes, and most importantly, around kitchen tables, let's explore how parents would get paid if they were to be paid. I'll refer to the proposal for paying parents as "parent comp."

Let's look at the following chart and accompanying rationale:

| Payor | Rationale |
|---|---|
| Employer / production company | Working conditions are made safer and more reliable. |
| Child | Working conditions are made safer. The risk of physical or emotional injury decreases. |

Following this rationale, should a "responsible adult" get paid in the parents' stead? (Those of you who are already veteran parents may confirm that this happens already.) If so, should the employer, the child, or the parent pay? You may feel strongly that since parents have a legal obligation to support their child, it should be the parent who pays with his or her money (not the child's earnings), most especially if a parent is working outside the home. Perhaps the costs should be shared in some fashion. Without a hard-and-fast rule, regulation, or law, figure on the "pay can" being kicked to the parent's or child's side since kids traditionally negotiate without much leverage, at least early on in their careers.

Especially for young children, some productions have, over the years, hired parents as assistants, hairdressers, and the like—with one notable hire being Shirley Temple's mother.

Finally, how much money are we talking about?

Although we risk offending parents who feel they are being dragged by their kids to audition after audition; who sacrificed their goals, paychecks, and personal time with family and friends; and whose contributions went or remain above and beyond the call for a dream their child desires, let's try to be objective about an hourly wage that might be earned by the sight and/or sound parent when the child is actually working weekly as a performer on an ongoing basis. If you are having difficulty grasping the kind of performer just described, think about a favorite television series of yours featuring kids, and then think about their performances on that set. Parent compensation may be a more palatable concept for some skeptics if we restrict our discussion to only those kids whose work schedules derail parents from working steadily in an existing job for which they are qualified and otherwise able to accept.

The US Bureau of Labor Statistics (BLS) reports median hourly wages of child care workers nationally, and as a basis for comparison, the online job search company Payscale, Inc., www.payscale.com, also lists such wages. (Be mindful that obtaining, compiling, and reporting by the BLS takes considerable time—generally about two years. Therefore, although those numbers reflect what the marketplace paid child care workers about two years ago, it's our starting point for discussion.)

| Hourly Wage | Annual Salary |
|---|---|
| $9.48[100] | $19,730[101] |
| $9.04[102] | $18,803[103] |

Now let's consider the concept of a floor. For the sake of discussion, let's reserve the parental compensation to parents of children who earn $200 gross or more in any given week for a commercial. This means that parents whose children earn $200 or less gross earnings don't get paid for their time.

Should parent comp be received solely by those parents who sit on sound stages or wait in designated areas, week after week, month after month, and longer as their kids work Broadway? What about parents who attend to their musical kids, essentially on a bus, from one city to the next as their child's music career careens across the States? Should they receive parent comp for being on that bus without any rehearsal or performance to supervise? Maybe that's okay with you. Should there be a ceiling or a cap that is reflective of a weekly salary of $379.20, based on the BLS hourly wage of $9.48 for forty

..................................................................

100 Bureau of Labor Statistics, "Occupational Outlook Handbook: Childcare Workers," US Department of Labor, January 8, 2014, www.bls.gov/ooh/personal-care-and-service/childcare-workers.htm.

101 Ibid. Refers to the median wage.

102 Average wage for childcare workers, www.payscale.com. Average wage regularly updated.

103 Ibid. Refers to the average wage.

hours per week (assuming, of course, that the parent actually worked forty hours) until the child's employment ends? Keep in mind that parent comp, if your tax advisor so advises, *could* be tax deductible as a paid expense. Deducting expenses from gross earnings adjusts the amount of money that must be paid in taxes.

Finally, consider parents who hire others to stand in for them at no less than $1,000 weekly with the money coming from the child's earnings. Perhaps that feels better for some of you who figure that $1,000 a week or $4,300 per month (because there are 4.3 weeks in a month) is a better deal because

- Mom or Dad continue to work outside the home, relying on that income to support the family;
- the weekly money paid may be far less than 15 percent of the gross;
- at least the money paid from the child's earnings benefits the child; and
- after seeking the advice of your tax advisor, parent comp *could* be considered a tax-deductible expense on the child's tax return.

From the child's view, Mom or Dad would be paid for their time but not overpaid at their expense.

There are no easy answers to these questions, but consider talking about them openly. Parent comp and related issues such as a parent paying his or her stand-in with the child's money is overripe for discussion.

*Note to parents:* During contract negotiations for a child's services, don't confuse parent comp with a producer's agreement to pay a parent's expenses for travel and associated accommodations when a parent accompanies his or her child to work "on location."

# CHAPTER 7

*Reality Shows*

Putting aside for the moment the enrichment of grown-ups through packaged reality shows that feature their kids, let's consider the question that is most asked about kids who appear in such shows. Why do parents place kids in a fishbowl for the amusement and profit of others? Instead of speculating on what makes some parents say yes to a producer who calls to "process the paperwork" that authorizes the filming of their child under eighteen for inclusion in a reality show, perhaps it makes sense to consider what kids receive or lose in the deal. That way parents who are considering allowing their child to be in a reality program will have a foundation from which to make an informed choice.

Reality shows are presently known in the industry as "unscripted programming." Production companies that create reality programs want to amuse and, in some instances, educate the public, but they also hope to make a profit from the enterprise. In turn, their business profits translate into taxable revenue on the federal, state, and local levels. Those profits also turn into personal income for workers who receive a paycheck or a cut—also known as points or percentages. Creators and producers of such shows rely on lawyers, accountants, and other financial professionals to assist them in advance of production to determine the most advantageous sites for filming—with the amount of money involved in each location being only one of many criteria considered. Experienced attorneys and other professionals who understand the interesting blend of state tax credits; labor, school, and entertainment laws; and child work permitting (if any) advise their clients on which state laws are "producer friendly." States without many, if any, restrictions or limit setting can become an integral part of that equation.

Not unlike other forms of television, the key to a reality show's success relates substantially to the number of viewers who watch it. Without enough viewers, the sale of airtime from advertisers to networks translates to lukewarm commercial success, if not cancellation. Without that success, the production company staff, cast, and crew who make the show go home. Consequently, reality programming thrives on drama, meltdowns, and sometimes humiliation, which may lead to a distortion of reality that promotes a pressurized environment.[104] "Children may inadvertently fuel the negativity because they feel pressured to entertain."[105] Further,

> an environment in which kids find themselves surrounded by cameras much of the time has the tendency to make the challenges of growing up much more difficult. Additionally, when competitive reality shows [include] children, there is added pressure and a sense of rejection when things don't work out. The Canadian newspaper "The Globe and Mail" reported in 2009 on a program called "The Next Star," which focused on kids under age 15, placing some contestants in embarrassing situations and leveling criticism (albeit constructive) at them on national television.[106]

........................................................................

104 See Laura Schlessinger, "Reality TV Is Child Abuse, Jon & Kate Plus 8," Newsmax, October 24, 2004, http://archive.newsmax.com/ archives/articles/2004/10/25/161525.shtml, cited in Dayna B. Royal, "*Jon & Kate* Plus the State: Why Congress Should Protect Children in Reality Programming," *Akron Law Review* 43 (2010): 435–500. See pp. 444–446.

105 Schlessinger, "Reality TV Is Child Abuse," cited in Royal, "*Jon & Kate* Plus the State," p. 445.

106 Kevin Bliss, "The Impact of Reality Shows on Children," LiveStrong .com, March 13, 2014, www.livestrong.com/article/228953-impact -of-reality-shows-on-children/#ixzz1UeH2Fl9h.

In analysis of reality TV shows, Aubree Rankin[107] writes that

> a growing consensus within the medical community that reality TV is bad for the contestants has arrived. Newcastle University (UK) psychologist Joan Harvey told the *Newcastle Journal* that she believes reality-show participants don't realize just what they're getting themselves into when they sign on to do these shows. "The contestants go into it with a certain amount of ambition but an awful lot of naivety [*sic*]. They are probably not as extrovert [*sic*] as they perceive themselves to be. They are more vulnerable than they think. . . . When your self-esteem does take a knock it can be quite catastrophic."[108] Indeed it can. One contestant voted off the original Swedish version of *Survivor* committed suicide a short time after

---

107  Aubree Rankin, "Reality TV: Race to the Bottom," Parents Television Council, n.d., www.parentstv.org/PTC/publications/reports/realitytv2/main.asp.

108  Will Mapplebeck, "How Reality TV Can Damage Your Health," Newcastle.co.us, October 24, 2003, quoted in Rankin, "Reality TV: Race to the Bottom."

he returned home, prompting the producers of many reality programs to keep psychologists on staff.[109]

When children sell their labor for entertainment, passionate argument ensues that they do so at grave personal expense. The core of these arguments places a mighty fine point on the erosion of humanity brought about by a child's exposure of his or her personal attributes way too soon. Aside from a child not being able to give informed consent, the preceding assessment is different for kids who appear or perform in reality television because they routinely do not get paid. Producers of this type of entertainment medium may maintain that children appear or participate in reality television but do not perform and, therefore, do not work. If they don't work, then there is no sale of a young person's labor. Consequently, state labor laws don't control and protect the child—or do they?

The New York State Department of Labor, which is empowered to regulate protections for child performers who either reside or work in New York State and their employers, recently added "an appearance in a reality show" to its definition of artistic or creative services of children. (Remember,

---

109 Erica Goode "Survivor's Nobler Roots: Psychologists Have Long Been Studying How Situations Influence Our Behaviour," *Gazette*, p. A6, August 27, 2000, cited in Rankin, "Reality TV: Race to the Bottom."

this issue was part of the kerfuffle that led to developing the new regulations.) About four years earlier, the *New York Times* reported that the highest court in France had ruled that participants on a French reality television show, *Temptation Island*, "were entitled to employment contracts and financial compensation—just as professional actors would be."[110] (Those reality stars reportedly scored paid overtime and holidays, too.)

What children say or do, without memorizing lines of dialogue from a script and presumably without direction, are bedrock reality components. Yet, whichever way you tilt the labor kaleidoscope, that child exhibited on camera arguably exposes 360 degrees of himself or herself. If the exhibition launches online, the exhibition becomes indelible and forever. If you think about the way you behaved when you were age seven and under extreme stress, would you want an instant replay button that lasts forever?

In the following discussion, "reality-based shows . . . [refer] to all real-time/live and/or documentary-style shows involving 'real people' or non-actors."[111] One particular show

110 Eric Pfanner, "The Reality of Reality TV: It's Acting, Court Rules," *New York Times*, June 7, 2009, www.nytimes.com/2009/06/08/business/media/08iht-reality.html?pagewanted=all&_r=1&.

111 Christopher C. Cianci, "Notes—Entertainment or Exploitation? Reality Television and the Inadequate Protection of Child Participants Under the Law," *Southern California Interdisciplinary Law Journal* 18, no. 363 (2009): 363–394, p. 384, footnote 156.

that aired on a network featured forty children, ages eight to fifteen, who were placed "in a New Mexico 'ghost town' for forty days, [to] see if they could build a working society without the assistance or guidance of adults, including their parents."[112] To be in the program, "the parents or legal guardians of the minors were required to sign, along with the children, a twenty-two page participant agreement."[113] Reportedly, Smoking Gun obtained a copy of the agreement from the New Mexico attorney general's office in response to its Freedom of Information Act Request:

> I understand that the Program will take place in . . . wilderness . . . over an extensive period of time. Accidents or illness may occur in remote places lacking access to immediate medical or emergency help and may be aggravated by exposure to temperature extremes or inclement weather. I understand that such conditions may impair or prevent the timely rescue of participants. . . . I understand that: (a) I will

---

112 Edward Wyatt, "CBS Was Warned on 'Kid Nation', Documents Show," *New York Times*, August 22, 2007, cited in Cianci, "Notes," p. 366.

113 "No Human Rights in 'Kid Nation,'" Smoking Gun, August 23, 2007, www.thesmokinggun.com/archive/years/2007/0823071kidnation1 .html, cited in Cianci, "Notes," p. 368. This section of the "Smoking Gun" article cites the Participant Agreement between Minor and Producers for the show's original title, "The Manhattan Project."

not be present with the Minor; (b) I will not have any means of direct or indirect communication with the Minor at all times during the Minor's participation in the Program which would prevent me from attending to the Minor's physical, emotional and mental needs; and (c) I acknowledge, understand and agree that the Producers will have my full permission and consent to oversee and supervise the physical, emotional and mental well-being of the Minor and to make all decisions during and in connection with the production of the Program on behalf of the Minor, including those decisions that may directly or indirectly affect the physical, emotional and mental well-being of the Minor."[114]

The agreement goes on to say that "the program . . . may cause the minor serious bodily injury, illness, or death" and that the parent "voluntarily and fully accepts and assumes these risks on behalf of the minor and himself/herself."[115] Yikes! There's more. The agreement required the parent to sign a $5 million liquidated damages clause if she or he or the child contacted the media without the "organization and sanction"

114 "No Human Rights in 'Kid Nation,'" Smoking Gun.
115 Ibid.

(that means permission) of the press officer or a duly authorized officer of the network. Bear in mind that this is only an excerpt. The rest of the agreement expands on rights that parents signed away.

Although it is fairly easy to get lost in the contract's details, consider what was reported to be happening on location. "The kids were divided into four . . . districts by the show's producers, and, every three days, the districts competed against each other on a physical or mental challenge, or a 'showdown,' the outcome of which determined their work and corresponding compensation for that episode."[116] One child who was able to take an interview reported that "the children . . . worked long hours—'from the crack of dawn when the rooster started crowing' until at least 9:30 p.m."[117] Whichever team came in last in the showdown "received 'laborer' status and earned ten cents for cleaning the entire town, including the portable toilets shared by all forty children."[118] A stipend of $5,000 was

........................................................

116 Maria Elena Fernandez, "Is Child Exploitation Legal in 'Kid Nation'? CBS Faces Barrage of Questions on a Reality Show about Children Fending for Themselves," *Los Angeles Times*, August 17, 2007, cited in Cianci, "Notes," p. 367.

117 Edward Wyatt, "A CBS Reality Show Draws a Claim of Possible Child Abuse," *New York Times*, p. B7, August 18, 2007, www.nytimes.com/2007/08/18/arts/television/18kid.html.

118 Fernandez, "Is Child Exploitation Legal in 'Kid Nation'?" cited in Cianci, "Notes," p. 367.

provided to most of the children "to cover incidental expenses but not as compensation for employment."[119] Other compensation for completing assigned tasks came in the form of "buffalo nickels," the town's currency . . . and gold stars worth $20,000 (and more), rewarded by the "kid government" to certain kids.[120] Furthermore, "complaints of cramped, unclean housing for the children, no adult supervision over potentially hazardous tasks, and physical injuries suffered by a few of the children while on set were made to New Mexico state officials. . . . Several children . . . required medical attention after drinking bleach left in an unmarked soda bottle, and one girl (11 years old) burned her face with splattered grease while cooking."[121]

So what do you think? I'd be interested to know what the parents who agreed to these terms were thinking.

The production ran from April 1 to May 10. Anne Henry, cofounder of BizParentz, a nonprofit organization that assists child actors and their families, spoke out. "I would . . . hope that the individual states where the kids are from . . . would . . .

----

119  Maureen Ryan, "What Were 'Kid Nation' Parents Thinking?" *Chicago Tribune*, September 4, 2007, cited in Cianci, "Notes," p. 368 and p. 372.

120  See Cianci, "Notes," p. 367, citing Fernandez, " Is Child Exploitation Legal?"

121  Wyatt, "CBS Was Warned," cited in Cianci, "Notes," p. 372, and Wyatt, "A CBS Reality Show Draws a Claim."

look into truancy issues. . . ."[122] The creator of the show, Tom Forman, said, "Because no tutors were on location, as is customary when children are hired for TV shows or movies, parents had to arrange with their children's schools to make up missed work."[123] One girl from Boston stated during an interview that "she missed 19 days of school and had 'to un-enroll from school and then re-enroll, so I didn't have to make up any work, which was awesome.'"[124]

The network maintained that its show was made in a "legal and ethical manner"[125] and that *no* laws were broken since "the children . . . 'were not working; they were participating' . . . and all were free to leave at any time."[126] The attorney general's office in New Mexico eventually carried out an official investigation, but "absent any formal complaints to [that] office or request for investigation by any state agency, [its investigation

........................................................

122 Maria Elena Fernandez, "State Attorney Probing 'Kid' Show," *Los Angeles Times,* August 24, 2007, http://articles.latimes.com/2007/aug/24/entertainment/et-kidnation24.

123 Ibid.

124 Ibid.

125 Maria Elena Fernandez, "Kids' Reality Show Fizzles Out: No 'Nation' and No Investigation," *Los Angeles Times,* December 5, 2007, cited in Cianci, "Notes," p. 374.

126 Fernandez, "Is Child Exploitation Legal in 'Kid Nation'?"

dropped.]"[127] Similarly, "the [New Mexico Department of Workforce Solutions] also dropped plans to investigate further into the matter."[128]

Since that time, circa 2007, the New Mexico legislature voted in legislation addressing a child's participation in front of the camera, which then-governor Bill Richardson signed into law. New Mexico is now one of a handful of states that require a mandatory Coogan account set aside (see Chapter 8, "And the Money Belongs to . . .") at 15 percent for minors.

Professionals in the social sciences, enraged by the reality television production niche as it involves children, criticize the medium openly. One clinician with whom I spoke (on the condition of anonymity) said that her child is not a child performer and that it will stay that way because she refuses to place her kid on a sound stage with other people in charge "who probably know nothing about how a child's psyche works."

Law colleagues and students, court staff and clients, family and friends consistently mention the same reality show about young girls competing in child beauty pageants. These people—younger and older, formally educated and life educated, stay-at-home parents and grandparents, together with

---

127  Fernandez, "Kids' Reality Show Fizzles Out," cited in Cianci, "Notes," p. 373.

128  Ibid.

aunts, uncles, cousins, psychologists, athletes, academicians, retirees, and so on—all say the same thing: "I hear you're writing a book about kid performers. Have you ever seen *that* show?" It surely strikes the proverbial nerve. *People* magazine reported the controversy with its cover story headline "Gone too far? Skimpy costumes, temper tantrums, pushy moms: A hit TV show ignites a furor over the shocking world of child beauty pageants."[129] Pageant parents say that winning is a real "confidence boost" for their daughters, with one mother reporting that her six-year-old was

> "retiring" from pageants . . . to pursue modeling. . . .
> Others insist that they're merely accommodating their
> children's desires—a claim psychologists dismiss as
> impossible at that age. . . . "This is the most blatant
> example of sexualization of a child that I have seen,"
> says Melissa Henson, director of communications and
> public education for the Parents Television Council,
> which is calling for the network to cancel the series.
> "There has to be a lesson here. This has gone too far."[130]

---

129  Charlotte Triggs, Kay West, and Elaine Aradillas, "Toddlers & Tiaras: Too Much Too Soon?" *People* magazine, September 26, 2011.

130  Triggs, West, and Aradillas, "Toddlers & Tiaras." Final production aired in 2013, but episodes remain accessible to online viewers.

When camera operators film long and winding temper tantrums, participating children distressed by long hours of preparation and associated stress, or parents dressing their children in extreme costumes, is there no responsibility taken for taking part?

*New York Times* columnist Frank Rich made the latter point beautifully in an editorial he wrote about a father and his then six-year-old son. Although Mr. Rich described a father "who mercilessly exploited his child for fame and profit,"[131] pointing out that about two million people watched the hoax unfold amid a "reigning culture, where 'news,' 'reality' television and reality itself are hopelessly scrambled,"[132] the trip-wire of a reality show's success is "the often voracious appetite of the viewing public for schadenfraude-ridden scandal."[133] In any event, parents aptly shoulder the precious responsibility of taking good care of their children.

So what do kids receive when they participate in a reality series? They receive a chance at fame, public identities, and

---

131 Frank Rich, "In Defense of the 'Balloon Boy' Dad," *New York Times*, October 24, 2009, quoted in Katherine Neifeld, "More Than a Minor Inconvenience: The Case for Heightened Protection for Children Appearing on Reality Television," *Hastings Communications and Law Journal* 32, no. 447 (Spring 2010): 458.

132 Rich, "In Defense of the 'Balloon Boy' Dad."

133 Rich, "In Defense of the 'Balloon Boy' Dad," cited in Neifeld, "More Than a Minor Inconvenience."

total exposure to "unscripted" participation without much, if any money, benefits, or the union protection that irons out minimum standards for the child's performance (e.g., wages and rules about hours that may be worked)—unless, of course, state legislators vote favorably on bills that demand regulation and governors sign that protection into law.

# Pageants

Distinguishing between televised reality programming featuring young children and more traditional pageant programs and classes preparing students with the skills necessary to walk onto a stage with confidence in an effort to secure the best possible outcomes for state- and national-level pageant interviews leading to scholarships should be a first stop for parents considering the pageant genre for their child. Some pageant students, over time, consider their evolving confidence, perspective, and sheer knowledge of lessons learned from quality preparation as irreplaceable *mojo*. Not all pageant programs and goals are the same, so peeling back the layers with recommendations is not to be skipped. Teachers, the curriculum, and stylized approaches can make all the difference in the life of a child.

# Parent Summary

If you are a parent, please make an honest and careful assessment about your son or daughter. Unscripted production can be a real minefield. Proceed with extreme caution. Contracts unfamiliar to you require translation by experienced lawyers. If you feel you do not have the money, even for a one-hour consult, a Volunteer Lawyers for the Arts committee may be able to help. Also, bar associations may offer reduced-fee panels involving lawyers who agree to work at a reduced rate. Beyond considering how you will be able to get good legal advice, consider how the demands and pressures of reality television will undoubtedly affect and complicate your family life. If you have other children, please take the time to make careful arrangements for them. If you believe that letting one of your children participate in a reality series will adversely affect him or her or your other children, or possibly your relationship with a spouse or partner, take the time to examine your motivations for considering the opportunity in the first place. (I have reviewed foreboding releases that include divorce in the list of claims that parents must waive for their child to participate.) Years from now, when episodes continue to be replayed on YouTube or are otherwise available online, will you regret your decision? Will your son or daughter be mortified? How will your decision affect your relationship with your son or daughter down the road? Consider the kinds of challenges and arguments that are likely to arise. For instance, when your child applies for a job fifteen years from now, going into a competitive job interview and projecting youthful vitality and confidence, will demoralization set in when he or she is asked about a captured humiliation? How will that make your child feel about those experiences and about you? As a parent, how will that make you feel, knowing that you gave your consent?

You have a lot to consider. After all, your child is trusting you. So don't miss the opportunity to make a thoughtful decision. Otherwise, rights can be signed away in perpetuity. That means forever.

# CHAPTER 8

*And the Money Belongs to . . .*

W hen a company hires a young performer under the age of eighteen to provide his or her artistic or creative services, who is lawfully entitled to his or her paycheck?

## Historical Context

If your hunch tells you that, historically, the parent's horse came in first to claim the funds, you are correct. Over the years, the law characterized this as parental entitlement.[134] This concept stretches way back to the Napoleonic Code. Not so different from how a servant's pay benefitted the master, a child's earnings helped keep the family afloat.

Parental entitlement remained, for the most part, the status quo right through the birth of the United States. Many colonial families in the New World farmed for a living. Consequently, a child's earnings on or off the farm were swapped for basic

---

134 The oldest male member of an agnatic family held "paternal power" and was thus entitled to the property of his minor offspring.

necessities. If the child worked someplace else, the father paid himself from what the child earned to compensate for the lost labor on the farm. This arrangement (wages in exchange for food, clothing, and shelter) evolved into American law. A father's obligation to support his children came with an entitlement to take the children's earnings. That rationale, interwoven into various state laws today, may give parents the right to sue for personal injuries and damages sustained by their child.

Some states adopted more progressive laws earlier than others when it came to kids. In fact, laws protecting a child's land or property (distinguishable from a child's earnings) cropped up in many state court decisions. One child from Illinois, for example, who was given money for enlisting in the army, got to keep it even though his father felt entitled to it.[135] Case law from Wyoming read this way: "A father is not entitled to any extraordinary gain of the child, or to profits arising from a sale, or to rents and profits derived from the occupancy of the child's land."[136]

That Wyoming decision, citing a Pennsylvania case from 1856, reasoned that the child's "right to be the owner of property is as clear and as well-protected as that of a person who

135 See *Magee v. Magee*, 65 Ill. 255 (1872).
136 *Kreigh v. Cogswell*, 45 Wyo. 531 (1933).

has arrived at full age. When anything is given to [a child] to be held . . . in his own right, he has the title to it, and the parent, guardian, or master has in law no more right to it (for any purpose beyond safekeeping) than a stranger."[137]

That 1856 case, by the way, was written more than 150 years before reality television followed another Pennsylvania family in a popular TV series. Labor permits, also known as work permits, were reportedly not issued for the young TV stars. This meant that their participation for hours on end was not considered work until the Pennsylvania Department of Labor and Industry stepped in.[138]

The Associated Press reported that the Pennsylvania Department of Labor and Industry decided that the kids should have had labor permits but that it would not take action against the producers, reporting as follows:

> The Department of Labor & Industry released a letter Wednesday to Figure 8 Films and Discovery Talent Services that outlines conditions under which it's resolving its investigation. The department says child-labor permits will be needed for any future

---

137 Ibid. citing *McClosker v. Cypher*, 27 Pa. 220 (1856).

138 The Commonwealth of Pennsylvania enacted the Child Labor Act in 2012.

filming and that a portion of the proceeds must go into a trust fund for the children.[139]

Substantial issues affecting children go beyond the money. The pressure to create hit shows also affects a show's agenda and with it, the kids.[140] Boundaries that would otherwise be in place for kids seem transient and, at best, like shifting sands when the ultimate goal is to keep a viewer from changing the channel. (See Chapter 7, "Reality Shows.") Consequently, a dedicated supporter who has the child's back is a necessity.

## Hollywood's Impact

Without a doubt, California boasts the most experience with child performers in the motion picture and television industries and, consequently, "the handling" of money earned by them. So not surprisingly, the state has earned its reputation of being a magnet for court cases involving child performers. However, some child performers who might have had reason to wind up in court did not do so, instead swerving away from

139  Associated Press, "'Jon & Kate Plus 8' Kids Should've Had Labor Permits, State Says," PennLive, April 14, 2010, www.pennlive.com/midstate/index.ssf/2010/04/jon_kate_plus_8_kids_shouldve.html.

140  See Royal, "*Jon & Kate* Plus the State," p. 445.

public battles with family members. With all of this came the overwhelming feeling that the law needed to change. "The notion that parents should own and control the token earnings of their children might have been appropriate at the turn of the century when a child's earnings would be of 'little value'" (from the 1800s to the early 1900s).[141] However, under the bright lights of modern-day America, the concept seemed pretty outdated and downright unfair.

Pent-up demand for change for children in California, which finally happened, can best be understood from stories of former child performers whose experiences taught them some pretty difficult lessons about the harsh realities of who owned the money they earned and the protections afforded them (or not afforded them) along the way. Across the street from the Los Angeles Superior Court, where I researched this book, as I turned a worn microfilm dial backward and forward, looking through a landscape full of allegations and defenses, Paul Petersen's insight about former child stars' inquiries to their parents upon discovery of what, if any, money was left for them, dogged me like a radio song, an earworm, that you just

......................................................

141  Mark R. Staenberg and Daniel K. Stuart, "Children as Chattels: The Disturbing Plight of Child Performers," *Beverly Hills Bar Association Journal* 32 (1997): 22.

can't get out of your head: "Did you love me for me or what I brought into this family?"[142]

## *Former Kid Stars*

Whatever protections are in place for young performers really began with Jackie Coogan. Jackie was born John Leslie Coogan on October 26, 1914, in Los Angeles, California. He died at the age of sixty-nine on March 1, 1984, in Santa Monica, California. You or someone in your family might best remember him as Uncle Fester of *The Addams Family*, a popular weekly television series circa 1964. Charlie Chaplin discovered him as a little boy dancing the shimmy in a Los Angeles vaudeville house. Coogan's father was a vaudeville actor, his mother a former child stage actress. As a young sprout, Jackie played Charlie Chaplin's sidekick in the movie classic *The Kid* (1918). Because of that movie's popularity, Jackie became a child actor "in demand." He appeared in the following films: *Peck's Bad Boy, My Boy, Oliver Twist, Trouble, Circus Days, Daddy, Long Live the King, Little Robinson Crusoe, Boy of Flanders, The Rag Man, Old Clothes, Johnny Get Your Hair Cut, Bugle Call, Buttons, Tom Sawyer,*

---

142 Petersen interview.

and *Huckleberry Finn*.[143] If you think that the 1980s pop musical track act New Kids on the Block put epoch merchandising on the entertainment map, think again. Jackie Coogan was heavily merchandised. Quite a commercial buffet fed off his name and image: dolls and figurines, records, toys, and even peanut butter were among the Coogan-branded items for sale.

Tragically, Jackie's father was killed in a car crash that also took the life of Jackie's best friend, Trent "Junior" Durkin, another young actor. Jackie was in the car at the time, but he survived. The day was May 4, 1935. Following the accident, his mother remarried. Although his mother's now almost legendary adherence to the letter of the law that Jackie's earnings belonged to her (and to her second husband) was no carefully guarded secret, the behind-the-scenes story of how the facts unfolded to result in a lawsuit is not nearly as well known and reads like a novel.

- According to the complaint in equity advanced by Jackie in 1938 against his mother and stepfather, Arthur Bernstein et al, by reason of Jackie's artistry and licensing of his name for merchandising, he *alleged* that "there was paid during Jackie's [sic] minority the approximate

........................................................

143 *John L. "Jackie" Coogan v. Arthur L. Bernstein, Lillian R. Coogan Bernstein et al.*, Superior Court of the State of California, for the County of Los Angeles.

sum of Four Million Dollars ($4,000,000.00)."[144] The now legendary young star further *alleged* that repeatedly during his childhood and before his father died, both Jackie's father and mother, in addition to Mr. Bernstein, told Jackie and others

> in substance, that everything that was being acquired from plaintiff's art and from the use of his name and all that had been so acquired in the past and all that might be so acquired in the future would be conserved, managed and held for the use and benefit of this plaintiff and would be turned over and delivered to plaintiff upon his attaining the age of twenty-one years. . . . [H]e was told that it was their intention that he should grow up like other boys and accordingly that he should be carefully limited . . . to an allowance of $6.25 a week for spending money; [Jackie] alleges that the counsel of his father . . . was unselfish devotion to his best interests [sic] . . . and with a genuine view to teach . . . him [sic] the conservation of assets and the value of money

......................................................................

144  Ibid.

> but that the said restrictions as carried out
> by the defendant [sic] and [Jackie's] mother,
> acting under the influence of the defendant
> [sic], after the death of [ Jackie's] father, were
> for selfish and ulterior motives.[145]

According to this court document and Jackie's *allegations*, Jackie's mother remarried on December 29, 1936 (about 19 months after Jackie's father died).[146]

- That before and by Jackie's twenty-first birthday, he received . . . in the way of property, nothing but the following:

    a.   his food

    b.   clothing

    c.   a college education

    d.   railroad transportation

    e.   one automobile . . . (valued at) [sic] $800

    f.   a place in which to live

    g.   several gifts from public admirers, among which were two platinum watches and a gold watch, one platinum watch . . . (worth) [sic] $2,500

    h.   $6.25 weekly in spending money

---

145  Ibid.

146  Ibid.

i. the payment of approximately $7,400 in premiums upon a life insurance policy

j. extraordinary amounts of cash on occasions such as his birthday and Christmas, never amounting to more than $50.00 and not aggregating in all more than $1,500.00

k. $1,000.00 in cash on the day before his [sic] twenty-first birthday[147]

- That on the day prior to his [sic] birthday, he was called into a conference with his mother and his step-father [sic] and he was given $1,000.00, which, it was stated, was a present to him; thereupon his stepfather [sic] stated that it was desirable to effect a change in connection with Jackie's [sic] policy of life insurance . . . to effect a reduction in the premium rate . . . and for this . . . purpose Jackie [sic] was asked to sign a document which he did; Jackie [sic] has since learned that the document in question was . . . direction and authorization to the Insurance Carrier to pay the surrender value of the said policy, amounting to more than $7,000.00, to his stepfather [sic] or his order.[148]

---

147  Ibid.

148  Ibid.

- On (his) [sic] twenty-first birthday his allowance of $6.25 a week was stopped and from and after that date he has received from his mother and stepfather [sic] absolutely nothing; that since his twenty-first birthday he has been living upon his own modest earnings as an actor.[149]

- Jackie [sic] alleges that on the day after his twenty-first birthday, he asked his mother and his stepfather [sic] when his money and property were to be turned over to him whereupon his mother, acting, Jackie [sic] verily believes, under the influence, domination and control of his stepfather [sic], stated to plaintiff, "You haven't got a cent," "There never has been one cent belonging to you, it's all mine and Arthur's" and "So far as we are concerned you never will get a cent."[150]

The court's voluminous file provided a pretty clear sight line into messy family wrangling from the 1930s that included a blistering defense by this mother and stepfather, a preliminary restraining order, and the appointment of a receiver to seize control of contested property. To give you a taste of the type of assets and property the receiver was ordered to hold on to

149  Ibid.
150  Ibid.

pending the court's say-so by judgment or order, consider this partial list: companies (e.g., Jackie Coogan Productions, Inc., and Coogan Finance Corporation), plus all assets of the Miller High Life Beer Co., including accounts receivable and a truck—the latter assets eventually delivered back to Mr. Bernstein by court judgment; life insurance, real estate, stock, and personal possessions such as fine jewelry; a 1938 Dodge station wagon; three Rolls Royce cars; and ten bottles and one can of beer. Eventually, judgments entered with particular property going to Jackie, but the epoch acrimony of that lawsuit endures. The spending could not be undone. The approximated sum of $4 million wasn't coming back. Reality set in.

It was reported by *Variety* that within forty-eight hours of Arthur Bernstein's declaration that "the law is on our side, and Jackie Coogan will not get a cent from his past earnings," the California legislature passed the so-called Coogan law.[151] The Coogan law added some beef to California's existing laws. It empowered judges with the authority to set aside up to 50 percent of a minor's net earnings. But what the right hand giveth, the left hand taketh away. Upon good cause shown (i.e., if you have a good enough reason that appears reasonable to the judge, he or she might change the trust or savings plan or kill it

........................................................................

151  Christopher Grove, "Coogan Law's Effectiveness Up for Debate," *Variety*, July 29, 1998.

all together), the trust could legitimately and legally evaporate. The money would likely go to the child's parents or guardian.

Before then, a 1927 law in California allowed judges to approve contracts signed by kids for acting or other dramatic services. Otherwise, the kids could walk away from contracts that did not provide support or care to them or their families. The judge's approval served as protection for the movie business because in the 1920s studios signed actors to exclusive contracts with options that could extend the contract for several years.[152] Why invest in a movie, and cast kids in roles, if the kids can change their minds halfway through shooting and go to either a competitor offering more money or home? That's too risky. Once a judge approved a minor's contract, the child was locked in.

Critics felt that Coogan's law did not offer enough protection for child actors. Since it was only voluntary to seek court approval, "if neither the producer nor the parent (sought) court approval of a contract, the child performers (were) denied any of the slim protections afforded them."[153] As a practical matter, kids who were signed to short-term contracts typically didn't

........................................................................

152  Ibid.

153  Staenberg and Stuart, "Children as Chattels," p. 27., cited in Ben Davis, "A Matter of Trust for Rising Stars: Protecting Minors' Earnings in California and New York," *Journal of Juvenile Law* 27 (2006): 71.

get the protection anyway. "Their employers (had) no incentive to seek court approval of these contracts because, due to their short-term nature (of the employment), there (was) little risk of disaffirmance."[154] Cast in a onetime role or in a TV commercial, the child's involvement began and ended in the blink of an eye.

## A Modern-Day Former Child Star

The tragic circumstances of a modern-day former child star may have turned out otherwise if, straight out of the gate, the court had initiated the appointment of an independent advocate to protect his interests. The grim financial picture of a former child star who debuted on a popular television show in the 1970s escalated to the point where he sued his parents and a business / investment management advisor. The complaint he filed with the court *alleged* the following:

- Breach of Fiduciary Duty
- Fraud
- Professional Negligence
- Constructive Fraud

........................................................................

154 Randy Curry, "The Employment Contract with the Minor Under California Civil Code Section 36: Does the 'Coogan Law' Adequately Protect the Minor?" *Journal of Juvenile Law* 7 (1983): 93–98, cited in Staenberg and Stuart, "Children as Chattels," p. 27.

- Conversion
- Money Had and Received
- Accounting
- Imposition of Constructive Trust[155]

Of significance, the young star *alleged* that his business / investment management advisor "exerted dominion and control over" his parents, influencing their decision making.[156] The defendants strenuously denied the allegations.

The sheer number of court documents dedicated to the fight between a son and his parents over money felt as unnatural to me as it appeared tragic, leaving me to wonder if even a semblance of a relationship could survive after a lawsuit of that magnitude. The torment of suing the very people who raised you must be one of those courageous life decisions that few people have the maturity, stability, or emotional and financial willingness and ability to take on, which is undoubtedly why so few kids sue.

................................................................

155 *Gary Coleman, an individual, Inc., and Ancha-Aquarius, Inc., a California Corporation, et al v. Anita DeThomas, an individual; DeThomas Bobo Associates, Inc., a California corporation; W. G. Coleman, an individual; and Edmonia Sue Coleman, an individual et al.* Superior Court of the State of California, for the County of Los Angeles.

156 Ibid.

In the end, the former child star prevailed. The judge, as reported, ruled that the star was entitled to a seven-figure award.[157] And yet, at least from the outside looking in, his life going forward appeared hard. He died at age forty-two.

## *A Typical Case of an Untimely Death of Coogan Accounts by the Internal Revenue Service and California Tax Board, or What Happens When Parents Don't Pay Their Kid's Taxes*

Bruce D. Sires is a trusts and estates attorney and partner of Valensi Rose, a boutique law firm in Los Angeles. This is a small portion of what he had to say during an interview with the *National Law Journal* about one child actor, her parents, and her money:

> I handled a case for one child. She came to me because the producers and the studio were concerned about how her parents were behaving on the set because it was disturbing the production. And Mom and Dad were handling the child's money and living very well with it. I set up a guardianship with the child with a

.......................................................................

157  See Shauna Snow, "People Watch," *Los Angeles Times*, February 24, 1993.

third party as the guardian. This woman was 16 years old at the time. And we got the money put aside for her. Unfortunately, during the time her parents were handling her money, they had never paid income taxes on the child's behalf. So when she turned 18, and she was now entitled to all this money, it came with a price tag because the [Internal Revenue Service] and the (California) Franchise Tax Board both came after her for the taxes for all the years she had been a child actress.[158]

When I caught up with Attorney Sires, he told me that, especially for such a terrific kid, the case was tragic. At the end of the day, the child had nothing, and her parents had nothing. When I asked how a young performer finds a specialized legal advocate of Bruce Sires's stature, he told me that "fortunately, the producers of her show were on a charities board that worked with abused children, who contacted Child Protective Services after witnessing mother's behavior on set. She was removed from mother's custody and [placed] with a relative. She needed a formal guardianship and the referral came to me that way. Her Coogan account went to pay her unpaid income

---

158  Amanda Bronstad, "Coogan Law Loophole Leaves Child Actors at Financial Risk," *National Law Journal*, April 18, 2011.

taxes and interest. The best we could do was waive penalties and reduce the interest owed. If you are a government, you must charge interest, but we persuaded them to reduce it."[159]

## *The Legendary Shirley Temple Black*

The late Shirley Temple Black did not sue her parents. Instead, she served as the United States Ambassador to the Republic of Ghana and a United States representative to the United Nations. She also became a mother and grandmother. Her death in 2014 at age eighty-six marked an epoch loss for America and the world.

In her elegantly written autobiography, *Child Star*, Black recounted the glory and grit of her early working years, which included several threats of kidnapping and a murder attempt. She wrote about relationships, her mother's love and care, and the complicated way her finances were "managed" by her father and others:

> Of my $3,207,666 of gross earnings, I retained $89,000, half in cash and half in a house (a backyard dollhouse). My rate of salvage was less than 3 percent over nineteen years effort.... Was the $44,000 balance

---

159  Interview with Bruce D. Sires, December 21, 2013.

all that remained from nine years of working for MGM and Vanguard? It seemed so little for so much work. I added up $891,067 of gross salary. As stipulated by the court, one-half went to my parents, outright. From the remaining half, I deducted taxes and the stipulated percentages for agent, school expenses, and business management. That left $356,000, the amount which my parents were ordered to have deposited in the trust. Yet it . . . contained $44,000. The more I checked my figures, the more inescapable became confirmation of my gnawing fear. For years Father had flagrantly disobeyed the Superior Court order. Commencing in 1942, he simply ceased depositing anything to my trust, a delinquency continued for eight years.[160]

When she finally reviewed her accounting records, she described what she saw:

Numbers meandered through an anthill of financial tunnels and switchbacks. Bank and brokerage accounts opened, multiplied, then vanished, while little Shirley earned, paid and supported. Baby bountiful from childhood, I purchased clothing, a parade of

......................................................

160   Black, *Child Star*, pp. 483–486.

automobiles, every dog bone, golf ball, and diamond for seventeen years. This had been my domain: parents, brothers, twelve household staff, until death a demanding grandmother, and two paternal uncles, whom I vaguely remembered collecting handouts at our gate. Implacably generous, I loaned cash, interest-free, to penitent friends of my parents and faceless names. . . . Few repaid. Summing up, I did.[161]

## California in the Twentieth and Twenty-First Centuries

The first decade of the new millennium witnessed the proverbial throwing of California's gauntlet when its legislature passed laws in 1999 and 2003 that cut off, at the knees, the century-old default that the money kids earned belonged to Mom and Dad.[162] Until then, the dusty law felt like it served as protection for employers on the contract side and parents on the money side during family entanglements, irrespective of the decade, making for tragic headlines through swarms of

........................................................

161  Ibid., p. 486.

162  To handle the issue, the California courts required parents to sign a quitclaim beforehand, acknowledging that money earned by the kids belonged to the kids.

accusations and very public pain. News organizations, sponsors, and the like were making money by reporting those train wreck stories while no work orders, so to speak, went out to fix the problems on the rails to prevent future crashes.

People wonder why change occurred at the turn of the twenty-first century. The old days of signing up droves of kids by the film studios were gone. Courts were seeing fewer long-term contracts that triggered a court-imposed set-aside. And who better to know this but grown-up child actors? Consequently, they endorsed the first of two sets of changes to the law sponsored by the Screen Actors Guild (SAG) through its Government Relations Department and Young Performers Committee, with then–guild president Richard Masur and coauthored by then–state senate president pro tempore John Burton and assembly members Sheila Kuehl (a former young performer of *Dobie Gillis* fame) and Scott Wildman.[163] Stars who lent their support included Paul Petersen, Melissa Gilbert, Brooke Shields, Malcolm-Jamal Warner, and Mimi Gibson, the latter a hardworking child actress who was reported to have been left penniless when she turned eighteen.[164] Active parents of current and former child performers also supported the

163  See Debra Kaufman, "Judicial Fix," *Hollywood Reporter Showbiz Kids Special Issue*, December 1999, p. 81.

164  Ibid.

cause. A team of dedicated people beyond those mentioned, in addition to the lawyers, turned the initiatives into law.

For more than twenty years, Barbara Rice, Esq., has served the families of Los Angeles County's Superior Court assigned to the Family Law Department, which includes families of child performers. Attorney Rice vividly remembered one of her first days at the court. "It was September 1993, the day after Labor Day," she recalled. "I received a call from a former actress who said that her parents physically, mentally, and sexually abused her. They said they spent all her money. But she heard that the court escrowed some of her money."[165] So this attorney tracked down whatever information she could glean from the court record, including the name of the lawyer who represented the studio who had signed the actress many years before. He remembered the case—it was one of his first as a young lawyer. Enlisting his cooperation, Rice pressed him to research the matter, which he did willingly. No happy endings for this actress, unfortunately. No trust money existed in escrow. "That woke me up," said Rice. "It showed me that my role was significant here, and that I needed to put into place a system at the court to protect those kids. Because of that actress, so many changes at the court have occurred."[166] She estimates that

................................................................

165 Personal interview with Barbara Rice, June 15, 2011.

166 Rice interview.

roughly a hundred child performer petitions come across her desk each month for review.

Enter Paul Petersen and the invitation he extended to Barbara Rice to attend a meeting of the Young Performer Committee at a time when he held affiliation with that union committee at SAG. The objective was to make the law more child friendly for young actors by fixing some of the problems (e.g., guaranteeing a payday for kids whether they worked three days or eight years—a payday that sadly did not happen for the wronged young actress previously discussed). As their work progressed, it became apparent that strong positions taken by parents, parent groups, the unions, other professionals in the know, and child advocates were hardly unified. In the end, cumulative knowledge honed from years of experience was offered by Rice, Sires,[167] and other industry legal counsel together with Paul Petersen, the guild, and others, including informed and enlightened legislators. This group worked to nail down certain protections for the core of the new law, then a cleanup bill. Some of the pivotal changes included the following:

........................................................................

167  Supported by the Beverly Hills Bar Association. See Kaufman, "Judicial Fix," p. 82.

1. Mother and father are no longer entitled to their child's earnings from artistic or creative services, sports performances, and the like.

2. Whether or not the contract gets approved by the court, 15 percent of a child's gross income must be set aside in a trust located in California. (That avoids a money chase across state or country lines, or even the Continental Divide.)

Although Attorney Rice maintains the common concern that the set-aside percentage should have been more, legal improvements for talented working kids were attained.

*Note about California law:* Even though some industry professionals feel that the forty-nine other states should adopt California's laws that apply to talented kids "lock, stock, and barrel," the message here isn't that every state should model its laws after those of California. To the contrary, each state has its own unique brand of laws already on the books and reflective of its spirit, culture, norms, residents, and resident industries as well as state sovereignty. New York, which boasts Broadway and the country's theatrical hub, serves as one illustrative example.

Lawmakers from states other than California might even point out that a concerted effort to take away a judge's power of discretion in California to award a set-aside greater than

15 percent succeeded (even amid that state's sophisticated and comprehensive set of laws and regulations). Simultaneously taken was the child's current or future expectancy of anything more than 15 percent by not requiring parents to set aside more.[168] Without considering family-specific parental resources, support obligations, and the anticipated incursion of business expenses, a hard-and-fast one-size-fits-all rule for every single child might fly in the face of existing state laws and protections afforded children in states other than California. Still, many states don't have much if any law to offer protection to talented working children (aside from work permitting regulations). In fact, existing laws of some states may not have kept up with widespread industry changes over time. Hopefully, that will change.

In California's defense and to its credit, all the money a child entertainer earns in California belongs to him or her. Even before the law effectively changed in 2000, the California Superior Court required parent(s) or guardian(s) to sign that quitclaim, whereby they would irrevocably and perpetually

........................................................................

168  Prior to 2003, the law in California read, "The court may require that *more than* [emphasis added] 15 percent of the minor's gross earnings be set aside in trust . . . upon request of the minor's parent or legal guardian, or the minor, through his or her guardian ad litem."

release and relinquish to the minor and lender[169] any interest they may have in and to all monies payable under the contract. (*Translation: Parents permanently handcuff themselves from asserting any right to their child's money.*) Kansas has also declared that the money belongs to the child. (Florida and Tennessee made the same declaration for their performing kids—with one major catch. To get it, court approval of the contract is required.)

Fifteen percent of gross earnings (e.g., $1,500 on a $10,000 paycheck) is put away until the young performer's eighteenth birthday[170] or until he or she is declared emancipated (see Chapter 12, "Emancipation: A Legal Escape Hatch for Kids"), if that happens before his or her eighteenth birthday. The year 2000 law pertains to all young performers and their contracts, not just those found to be court approved. The second round of changes (cleanup) in 2003 added the requirement that the 15 percent trust set-aside must remain in California. Money cannot move out of the state or out of the country for that matter.

Here are two final facts:

---

169 *Lender* references a loan-out corporation if one is established for the minor's benefit.

170 See Chapter 14 for states that follow or deviate from this protocol.

1. Barbara Rice has constructed and maintains a website dedicated to the how-tos of the petitioning process for minor contracts at the Los Angeles Superior Court. She has also created court forms that employers and families continue to use.[171]

2. From the 1940s through the 1970s, the set-aside was made through the purchase of US savings bonds and held in the court's vault until the young performer turned twenty-one. After Barbara Rice joined the court as a research attorney, she discovered several bonds belonging to former young performers. With Paul Petersen's guild contacts and assistance, she pledged that those bonds would go to their rightful owners. Today, unclaimed bonds are still in that court's vault! Visit Barbara Rice's website and click "Bonds" for more information.[172]

## The Law in Action: Seeing Is Believing

Let's consider the following case:

---

171 See "Minors' Contracts" at www.home.earthlink.net/ ~minorscontracts/index.html.

172 Rice interview.

The parents of the performers owned a company. Let's refer to their company as POP LLC. The parents served as producers who would produce and record their kids' music. The kids were the musicians, singers, songwriters, and performers. Everyone signed the contract. All the kids were under the age of eighteen. Petitions seeking contract approval were filed with the court. Remember, a contract signed by parties (including the minor) is reviewed at that time. If and when a judge at the court approves the petition, it is as if the child signed the contract as a grown-up. He or she can no longer claim minority status ("I wasn't eighteen, so I wasn't old enough to know better") as an excuse to get out of the deal. Instead, he or she must fulfill all obligations and responsibilities. He or she will reap the benefits, too.

So what did the court do? Drumroll, please . . .

The court denied the petitions, meaning the court refused to approve the contract that goes with the petitions. But the court did so "without prejudice." (This means the parents could refile the petitions with revised contracts at a later date after changes were properly made.) The following summarizes the court's ruling and rationale:

- The court was concerned that there may not have been arm's-length negotiations between the contracting parties because (a) POP LLC's managing member was the father of one of the minors, (b) the court was informed that other members of POP LLC were also parents of the minors, and (c) the minors were not represented by independent legal counsel during contract negotiations. *Translation: The minors weren't negotiating on a level playing field. Since three parents held ownership interests in the company contracting with the kids, the deck was stacked against them. Consequently, they needed independent legal advice.*

- There appeared to be a conflict of interest between each minor and his or her guardian ad litem (parent) since POP LLC failed to show that the guardians ad litem had no interest in the production agreements. *Translation: The kids' guardians ad litem are the parents who own the production company contracting with their children. Therein lies an apparent conflict of interest.*

- By contract, the minors gave POP LLC a 40 percent cut of all compensation payable to them, as well as a 50 percent interest in compositions written by them. There was no obligation on the part of POP LLC to produce a record under the production agreements. POP LLC was merely lending out the minors' services. The court ruled that it was not in the best interest of the minors to sign these particular contracts. *Translation:*

*The parents asked for too much money and property (music ownership), and the kids were bargaining for the short end of the stick without being guaranteed a record.*

So what happened next? The kids' parents sought out an experienced entertainment attorney to represent their kids as a negotiator and serve as their guardian ad litem.[173] Although I won't tire you with the details, the kids got a much better deal the second time around. Having an independent advocate generally has that effect. Consequently, the court approved the newly revised contract and ordered that 15 percent of the gross earnings payable to each minor by POP LLC be deposited into one or more Coogan trust accounts with the parent(s) serving as trustee(s) for their son or daughter.

The preceding scenario is unusual. Court counsel explained that when the court denies petitions, most people won't return with revised and amended agreements in tow. The parents, in this instance, should be credited for that.

---

173 State laws vary on the permissibility of this dual role.

# CHAPTER 9

*How Kids Get Out of Contracts:*
*Disaffirmance*

In substance, a child can legally walk away from a contract she or he signed, leaving the other person or entity high and dry. (There may be particular state exceptions to this rule, but you get the drift.) Although you may not think about it in these terms, a child, until he or she reaches the age of majority (now generally eighteen, formerly twenty-one), cannot under ordinary circumstances buy a car, boat, or even a time-share since he or she is considered, by law, too young. Essentially, a child's limited capacity to understand legal rights and obligations offers him or her a free pass from legal entanglements brought on too early in life. Below is a Q&A addressing some questions you might have.

Q: Is there a federal law regulating work standards for children who act or perform in motion pictures or theatrical productions, or radio or television productions?

A: No.

Q: Why not?

A: The Fair Labor Standards Act (FLSA) of 1938 makes it unlawful for an employer to use "oppressive" child labor.[174] But Congress carved out an exception for actors or performers.

Minors employed as actors or performers in motion pictures or theatrical productions, or in radio or television productions are exempt from the FLSA coverage. Therefore, FLSA rules regarding total allowable number of work hours in one day and allowable times of day to work do not apply.[175]

Q: Why doesn't the FLSA protect these child performers?

A: That is an excellent question, and answering it requires some understanding of history. At the time of the Great Depression, "only 50 percent of teenagers finished high school."[176] A quarter million teenagers left home. "Teenage hoboes were roaming America . . .

174 29 USC § 201 et seq.

175 See US Department of Labor, "Youth & Labor: Entertainment Industry Employment," n.d., www.dol.gov/dol/topic/youthlabor/entertainmentemployment.htm.

176 Committee on the Health and Safety Implications of Child Labor; Commission on Behavioral and Social Sciences and Education; Division of Behavioral and Social Sciences and Education; National Research Council; Institute of Medicine, *Protecting Youth at Work*, Washington, DC: National Academies Press, 1998, p. 47, cited in Seymour Moskowitz, "Save the Children: The Legal Abandonment of American Youth in the Workplace," *Akron Law Review* 43 (2010): 111, www.uakron.edu/dotAsset/929338.pdf.

with the blessing of parents or as runaways, they hit the road and went in search of a better life."[177] In the early 1900s and leading up to the Great Depression, "child labor had become a widespread problem in the United States."[178] Some children invariably ended up working as child actors or "extras" in Hollywood.

Not surprisingly, President Franklin Delano Roosevelt proposed to Congress, "federal regulation to solve the problem of child labor and set minimum wages and maximum work hours."[179] However, a ban on all child labor would have made child acting unlawful. So an exception for child actors and performers was carved out. In addressing the issue, Congress looked at Shirley Temple's career specifically and realized that "an outright ban on all child labor would have made [her] acting career illegal."[180] During the dark days of the Great Depression, her extraordinary talent

177 Errol Lincoln Uys, *Riding the Rails: Teenagers on the Move During the Great Depression*. New York: Routledge, 2003, p. 1.

178 Hugh D. Hindman, *Child Labor: An American History*. Armonk, NY: M. E. Sharpe, 2002, cited in Ang, *Teenage Employment Emancipation*, p. 402.

179 John S. Forsythe, "Legislative History of the Fair Labor Standards Act," *Law and Contemporary Problems* 6 (1939): 464–466, cited in Ang, *Teenage Employment Emancipation*, p. 403.

180 Ang, *Teenage Employment Emancipation*, p. 404.

held special meaning because it entertained troubled audiences. So in addition to the enrichment of society via performances by Shirley Temple and others, child acting was also beneficial to the economy[181] (e.g., more movies, more tax revenue). Consequently, Congress made it clear that child acting was not "oppressive child labor."[182]

Q: Is that why the federal law is sometimes referred to as the "Shirley Temple exception"?

A: Yes.

Q: So some states have laws that affect child labor in the entertainment and sports industries and other states don't?

A: Yes. Congress has left it up to each state to make laws for its residents. State education laws, however, should extend to all young people, whether or not they can sing, dance, or otherwise perform or work.

Q: Is each state law or set of laws the same?

A: No, although some states may borrow language from other states. State laws vary with respect to what types of contracts minors sign that are enforceable and under what circumstances. This is why the United

..........................................................................

181 See ibid., p. 405.

182 Ibid.

States currently has a "patchwork quilt" of state laws. See Chapter 14, "Tables and Resources" for a listing of certain state laws pertaining to child performers.

Q: Once a state court judge approves a contract, can a child performer walk away from the contract he or she has signed?

A: No.

Q: Are there any exceptions to that last answer?

A: It depends on the circumstances and the state. Some state laws clearly delineate that a child must honor the contract. Other state laws may direct that if a child was defrauded or otherwise harmed or injured, a judge may permit contract revocation or release the child from the contract. This means that the court can set aside its earlier approval and permit the child to walk away from the contract without it being enforced against the child. But technically, that circumstance does not add up to disaffirmance. Either way, if you are a working minor and feel that you are in harm's way, seek professional help immediately.

Q: Should a minimum uniform standard be established to protect children in all fifty states?

A: Definitely. A federal law that sets forth, at the very least, a minimum threshold of protection for working child performers is long overdue for enactment. That way, children who reside or work in states without any laws or regulations in place will at least receive minimum protection. Children who reside or work in states with stricter standards will continue to receive the enhancement.

# CHAPTER 10

*Parent Agreements*

A parent's entrée into the land of parent agreements may go something like this:

A casting agent calls and says, "We would like Megan to read for the part of Samantha." The parent drives Megan to read. Megan goes into a room, and the door closes. Fifteen minutes later, Megan comes out.

Mom asks, "How did it go?"

Megan replies, "Fine."

A week goes by. A second call comes in from the same casting agent. "We would like Megan to come back to read for the part of Samantha." The parent drives Megan back to read. Megan goes back into the same room, and the door closes. Twenty minutes later, Megan comes out.

Mom asks, "How did it go?"

Megan replies, "Fine."

Two weeks come and go. A third call comes in from the same casting agent. "We would like Megan to come back in to read for the part of Samantha again." The parent drives Megan back again to read. Megan goes into the same room, and the door closes. Twenty-five minutes later, Megan comes out.

Mom asks, "How did it go?"

Megan replies, "Fine. Someone else was in the room. It was the director."

Mom didn't know that the director would be there this time. An hour later, Mom's cell phone rings. Megan got the part. Mom is told that contracts will be faxed to her for Megan to sign. Mom is also told that parent agreement(s) will be faxed to her and that they should be signed immediately and faxed back.

## The Legal Skinny About Parent Agreements

Court filing of contracts for minors, once approved, protects companies and others who contract with young performers from disaffirmance by the young performer. (See Chapter 9, "How Kids Get Out of Contracts: Disaffirmance" for a Q&A about disaffirmance.) Companies hiring kids typically require parents to sign a parent agreement, regardless of whether a contract gets filed and approved. The "What if a kid changes his mind?" problem, especially for those companies who either avoid the court approval process altogether or don't have one in their state, underscores the importance of getting a parent or parents to sign one. From the company's perspective, think about these agreements the way you would think about insurance. If a company car becomes unusable, the insurance company pays. A similar principle is at play here, except the child's performance, for whatever reason, isn't happening.

## *What Do Parent Agreements Do?*

Generally, agreements require parents to guarantee the following:

- Their child's performance
- That they will cover all company costs, including attorneys' fees and costs, if their child fails or refuses to perform

*Note to parents:* No matter how much gold or silver a person can fetch from his or her wallet, the threat of paying the other side's legal fees and costs provides strong motivation and incentive to both parents and children to make sure that the child performs pursuant to the contract.

Some of you reading this with working kids already may feel prompted to dash to your contracts folder to see if you too were required to sign a parent agreement and to subsequently read, perhaps for the first time, what it says. Although parent agreements vary, the following language typifies the crux of the parental hook:

- The parent(s) has read the contract, line by line, understands it, and is satisfied that the contract is fair, just, and equitable and for the minor child's benefit.

- The parent(s) agrees, represents, and guarantees that during the contract term the minor will perform his or her services under the contract, the minor will observe and perform each and all of the obligations of the contract, and the minor will not disaffirm the contract.

- The parent(s) agrees that if the minor fails to observe or perform any or all of his or her obligations under the contract, the parent will perform the minor's obligations (e.g., if the minor is obligated to pay someone a commission, then the parent is obliged to pay the commission).

- The parent(s) agrees that if the minor fails to observe or perform any or all of his or her obligations under the contract, the parent shall indemnify and hold harmless the company and the company's successors and assigns from and against any and all damages, costs, liabilities, or expenses including reasonable attorney's fees arising from minor's actions.

*Note:* This last paragraph basically commits a parent to pay for everything that can be documented and proven as a damage or expense (e.g., advanced by a lawsuit).

Now ask yourself the following questions:

- Do the terms of this parent agreement bother you?

  If your answer is "Yes," you are not alone. Guaranteeing any person's performance, whether or not they have reached eighteen years of age, is like forcing a person to work.

- What happens when the contract is a reality television contract and the child is not being paid?

  Leaving aside the thorny issue of whether a child's participation in reality programming is work (see Chapter 7, "Reality Shows"), forcing a person to participate in an unpaid venture feels like a violation of the prohibition against slavery.

- What if the child or parent feels justified in putting on the brakes and going home?

  Ideally, reasonable people can resolve their differences amicably without trumping the court card. (The operative word in the last sentence would be *ideally*, as court dockets remain filled to the brim with the reasonably minded.) Otherwise, state laws may allow a parent to go back to court (if the court's approval was granted in the first place) and have the court's approval revoked if proof exists that the child's best interests are being jeopardized (e.g., the child has been or is being harmed, injured, and/or damaged in some way). If and when that occurs, the company's legal fees paid to oppose that action could then be lumped into its demand that the parent pay for those expenses, too. Whether the company will win is another matter entirely.

## For Legal Eagles

In one particular case involving an underage model, a New York court refused to uphold a parents' guarantee for their daughter's performance.[183] That court ruled that the written contract did not comply with New York law requiring the underage model to "secure a work permit"[184] and that her employment "be in accordance with the rules and regulations promulgated by the Commissioner of Education."[185] The court also ruled that

......................................................................

183  See *Metropolitan Model Agency USA, Inc. v. Rayder*, 168 Misc. 2d 324, 643 N.Y.S.2d 923 (Sup. Ct. NY Co. 1996).

184  Ibid.

185  Ibid.

the parents were not liable on their guarantee, finding it void as an attempt to circumvent New York law. New York's strong public policy of protecting minors, leading to numerous laws designed to protect them from adult exploitation, was cited in that decision.

Every parent should take the time to think about the following questions and their answers before signing a parent agreement:

1. Do I understand what this agreement says?

2. Do I have the information necessary to make an informed decision?

3. What wiggle room exists to alter the terms to make the agreement more parent and child friendly?

4. Am I willing to guarantee my son or daughter's performance and pay the company its losses, damages, and legal fees if my son or daughter doesn't perform or participate? Am I willing to fight to kick the guarantee to the curb at a later date?

5. Am I willing to place the company's financial health and investment before my son's or daughter's needs or desires?

Finally, if you are a parent reading this, please stop to appreciate the distinction between the entertainment industry's standard use of parent agreements to protect its investments and your personal standards as a parent working to meet your son's or daughter's needs and protect his or her best interests.

# CHAPTER 11

*Taxes—Especially for Parents*

Benjamin Franklin once said, "The only things certain in life are death and taxes." Assessing the fairness of a 15 percent set-aside, compared with other percentages, begins with an understanding of tax rates. I know—I'm making you groan, aren't I? So I'll make a deal with you. I will do my very best *not* to write a boring chapter (because I figure few of you will actually read it) if—and this is a big *if*—you will pay attention to some basic information, a few charts, and a top ten list. If we have a deal, read on. Otherwise, you can skip this, but don't say I didn't warn you.

*A golden rule:* Find the right tax professional with experience working with entertainers or athletes. Ask for current references from people who have similar situations and concerns. In addition, ask about costs and the professional's client communication policy (e.g., "How much do your services cost, and how long will it take to receive a return e-mail, text, or call?"). Why? The entertainment business is unique. Tax preparers accustomed to reading and working with royalty statements (residual and otherwise) and production and distribution company statements, as well as those who claim back-of-the-hand familiarity with the records needed for complete tax preparation can make or break that familiarity with the records needed for complete tax preparation.

The sports industry includes several unique features, too. At times, the industries blend when career success includes income streams from both worlds. Some tax preparers hold the certified public accountant (CPA) credential, but others do not. In addition, not all CPAs prepare tax returns. Please do your homework carefully and select the right person for the job. Look behind "the amazing" brand (e.g., "Sam is amazing! There is nobody better."). Similarly, a CPA firm may enjoy a solid reputation, which is great, but what you need to know is which accountant in that firm will actually be working with you. Is that person experienced handling clients just like your son or daughter? Is he or she compatible with your child's needs as well as yours? Of crucial importance, will he or she be accessible to you? *Translation: How quickly will he or she respond to your e-mail or a phone call?* By way of analogy, think about selecting a doctor or lawyer. The hospital or law firm with which the doctor or lawyer is affiliated may enjoy a stellar reputation, but the doctor or lawyer, although skillful, may possess little in the way of interest, empathy, or compassion and, therefore, may not be the right choice.

Here's the nitty-gritty on what tax advisors can do for you:

Customary and legitimate expenses that may be reported as deductions on tax returns are significant. So a savvy professional can be worth his or her weight in gold if able to make sense of the plethora of expenses that may or may not be deducted from earned income and advise you accordingly.

Beyond tax preparation, skilled and experienced accountants (in conjunction with the right lawyer) can advise the client on the right tax structure. A question like "What are the pros and cons of my child remaining self-employed as opposed to establishing a corporation for my child?" should be routine for the skilled professional to answer. An earnest and easy to understand discussion about the type of corporation or partnership status that might be established similarly ranks high on a must-do list.

A written professional services agreement, if you are asked to sign one, can be good for everybody as long as the terms and rates are fair and reasonable. If you don't know what "fair and reasonable" is with respect to the sort of professional you are hiring, ask around. Tax season comes once a year, giving you plenty of time to explore, do your own research, and select the right pro in advance.

Any federal and state taxes owed by your child must be paid if and when due—and that means on time. Do not assume that your child's manager or agent will do this. In fact, the general rule of service agreements (e.g., personal management and agency contracts) is that they say just the opposite. Your child is responsible for paying federal taxes, and if he or she is working in a state where taxes are collected, he or she must pay state taxes, too. (Professional athletes and entertainers customarily file several state tax returns in the states where they live, play, and work. This also holds true for talented kids who tour from state to state.) On or about April 15 is usually (but not always) the last day tax returns may be filed for individuals. It's usually on or about March 15 for corporations, but those dates do vary from year to year. Please check with an experienced tax preparer to guide you on the drop dead date for filing. If a tax return is not filed and payments owed are not submitted, your child can look forward to the accrual of penalties and interest. This can be devastating to working kids, especially if their parent(s) spent or relinquished control of all the money their child earned, with the only asset left being the trust or set-aside account(s).

*Note to parents:* Your child's tax returns must be prepared and filed on or before a particular date but—and this is a big *but*—gathering the information should be a year-round system instead of a chaotic and panic-laden last-minute drill.

An overarching reason behind the set-aside fixed by the state of California at a modest 15 percent rests, in large part, with concerns that when Los Angeles Superior Court set the bar at a 30 percent gross for the set-aside (some years back), some families and other pros argued that woefully little money was left for walking around. Assuming that the kids were paying for an agent and a manager and paying taxes in the 40 percent range, the grouse for these higher-bracket earners was that only crumbs remained for them.

## Taxes

Income taxes get paid on moneys earned after deductions and exemptions. Fees for agents, managers, and lawyers may be deducted under the tutelage of a specialized accountant. For all children working in the United States, no hard-and-fast rules exist about the percentage of tax kids pay based on the money they earn. Essentially, federal and state income taxes owed (if the state collects income tax, which some states don't) are calculated against net income. Experienced pros are valuable because they figure out what *net* means after taking into account exemptions and deductions. Rest assured of a universal tax truth though—East Coast to West Coast—that whether a person is selling doughnuts, acting, modeling high-end stilettos, or exhibiting athletic prowess, paying taxes comes down to income reporting, deductions, and exemptions. How much your child will pay and when should be based on the advice of your tax advisor.

According to William J. Austin, a veteran CPA with twenty-six years of experience advising individuals and small to mid-size businesses and currently a director at Marcum LLP:

> The safe bet is that depending on the income level, the combined federal and state tax levels will generally fall between 10 percent to 40 percent of net income. In some instances, no tax will be owed and, in others, a smidge over 40 percent may occur. You get to deduct your ordinary and necessary business expenses like management, agent, and legal fees. It is further complicated by organizational structure, whether the child is self-employed or set up to be an employee of his or her own company. If a child is an actual employee of a touring company and he or she receives a W-2 at the end of the year showing lower income levels, his or her agent and management fees may not yield a tax deduction. Being claimed a dependent on parents' tax

returns will also affect the bottom line. But remember that in order for a parent to declare a child as a dependent, the parent must contribute more than 50 percent to the child's support.[186]

Whether or not kids pay a 40 percent income tax (state and federal) or 15 percent, the set-aside in California and some other states mirroring California is 15 percent. As of 2014, the highest federal rate is 39.6 percent for income over $406,750 for a single filer, with the tax breakdown looking like this:

## Taxable Income

| $ Over | $ Not Over | Tax Percentage |
|--------|-----------|----------------|
| — | 9,075 | 10.0% |
| 9,075 | 36,900 | 15.0% |
| 36,900 | 89,350 | 25.0% |
| 89,350 | 186,350 | 28.0% |
| 186,350 | 405,100 | 33.0% |
| 405,100 | 406,750 | 35.0% |
| 406,750 | — | 39.6% |

A parent's responsibility to pay whatever taxes are owed by his or her child, on time, should be neither a surprise nor a

186 Personal interviews with William J. Austin, November 20, 2012, and April 10, 2015.

hardship, especially for those kids taxed at the lower or $0 rate. It adds insult to injury when this does not happen, prompting sometimes a "trust bust" and liquidation of the set-aside. Trust busting occurs when a parent legally seeks access to the trust money, generally before the minor's eighteenth birthday. It's a legal way, if court approved, of emptying a child's piggy bank or safe.

Check out the following charts prepared by Austin and based on 2014 tax rates.[187] These three charts reflect federal and California state tax owed from gross pay earned at $10,000, $100,000, and $500,000. Pay special attention to net cash dollars. *Note:* This information is based on 2014 tax rates. Parentheses indicate negative values.

---

187  Prepared without including and factoring other "ordinary and necessary" expenses that may be considered tax deductible.

# Tax Chart Showing Gross Pay at $10,000

| Dependent on Parents' Return | | YES | | NO |
|---|---|---|---|---|
| Gross Pay | | $10,000 | | $10,000 |
| Less Deductible Business Expenses | | | | |
| Agent | $1,000 | | $1,000 | |
| Manager | $1,500 | | $1,500 | |
| Legal | $1,000 | $3,500 | $1,000 | $3,500 |
| Net Before Taxes | | $6,500 | | $6,500 |
| Higher of State Tax or Standard Deduction | | $6,200 | | $6,200 |
| Exemption | | — | | $3,950 |
| Deduction for 50% of Self-Employment Tax | | $459 | | $459 |
| Taxable Income | | ($159) | | ($4,109) |
| Federal Tax | | — | | — |
| Self-Employment Tax | | $918 | | $918 |
| State Tax (CA) | | $20 | | $20 |
| Net Cash | | $5,562 | | $5,562 |
| Tax Rate on Gross Income | | 9.384% | | 9.384% |

# Tax Chart Showing Gross Pay at $100,000

| Dependent on Parents' Return | | YES | | NO |
|---|---|---|---|---|
| Gross Pay | | $100,000 | | $100,000 |
| Less Deductible Business Expenses | | | | |
| Agent | $10,000 | | $10,000 | |
| Manager | $15,000 | | $15,000 | |
| Legal | $10,000 | $35,000 | $10,000 | $35,000 |
| Net Before Taxes | | $65,000 | | $65,000 |
| Higher of State Tax or Standard Deduction | | $6,200 | | $6,200 |
| Exemption | | — | | $3,950 |
| Deduction for 50% of Self-Employment Tax | | $4,592 | | $4,592 |
| Taxable Income | | $54,208 | | $50,258 |
| Federal Tax | | $9,413 | | $8,425 |
| Self-Employment Tax | | $9,184 | | $9,184 |
| State Tax (CA) | | $2,756 | | $2,756 |
| Net Cash | | $43,647 | | $44,635 |
| Tax Rate on Gross Income | | 21.353% | | 20.365% |

# Tax Chart Showing Gross Pay at $500,000

| Dependent on Parents' Return | | YES | | NO |
|---|---|---|---|---|
| Gross Pay | | $500,000 | | $500,000 |
| Less Deductible Business Expenses | | | | |
| Agent | $50,000 | | $50,000 | |
| Manager | $75,000 | | $75,000 | |
| Legal | $50,000 | $175,000 | $50,000 | $175,000 |
| Net Before Taxes | | $325,000 | | $325,000 |
| Higher of State Tax or Standard Deduction | | $25,003 | | $25,003 |
| Exemption | | — | | $2,054 |
| Deduction for 50% of Self-Employment Tax | | $11,606 | | $11,606 |
| Taxable Income | | $288,391 | | $286,337 |
| Federal Tax | | $83,043 | | $83,043 |
| Self-Employment Tax | | $24,113 | | $24,113 |
| State Tax (CA) | | $26,779 | | $26,779 |
| Net Cash | | $191,065 | | 191,065 |
| Tax Rate on Gross Income | | 26.787% | | 26.787% |

Next, we connect the dots between net cash and the 15 percent set-aside for the minor in the preceding tables.

## Net Cash Without Factoring the Minor's Set-Aside or Deductible Expenses

| Gross Pay | Gross Pay Set-Aside for Minor | Net Cash[188] |
|---|---|---|
| $10,000 | $1,500.00 | $5,562 |
| $100,000 | $15,000.00 | $43,647 or $44,635 |
| $500,000 | $75,000.00 | $191,065 |

As you can see, the higher the income, the larger the difference between the set-aside and net cash received.

## A Common Argument

The intensity of expenditure, for example, of parents who move with their child to New York City for their child's "once-in-a-lifetime opportunity" may likely argue that the exorbitant cost of living and travel leaves little in the way of savings. (Some people have located to New Jersey instead of New York City, electing to commute by train to save money.) Other parents with the good fortune of being spared pricey relocation costs and who pay lower living costs may be presented with the opportunity of putting away far more than 15 percent.

..........................................................

188  Without factoring any reduction for either the set-aside or other deductible expenses.

With the proviso and understanding that ordinary and necessary expenses associated with professional success may reduce both taxes owed and the savings that parents can justifiably put away for their child, which underscores the need for a proven tax advisor, please take special care of your son's or daughter's earnings.

Now, one final missive: a parent's duty to support his or her son or daughter does not generally go away if the child is working. Taking permissible deductions of certain expenditures does not change the parent's obligation by law.

Speaking of New York, consider this interesting wrinkle. "The New York State personal income tax return required for an individual who is unable to make a New York State personal income tax return by reason of minority . . . must be made and filed by his guardian . . . fiduciary, or other person charged with the care of his person or property (other than a receiver in possession of only a part of his property), or by his duly authorized agent. In such a case, the fiduciary or other person charged with the care of his person or property is liable for the income tax."[189] *Translation: If you are a guardian or fiduciary charged with the care of a talented working minor and/or his or her property,*

---

189  20 NYCRR §151.12. See also NY CLS Tax §651(d).

*and if that minor must file a New York State personal income tax return, the responsibility for preparing and filing the return rests on your shoulders.* This regulation may be especially helpful when a minor is faced with a tax lien on his or her earnings. Therefore, please consult a specialized attorney and tax advisor well versed in New York law and regulation and your particular circumstances to advise you as regards *your responsibility and liability.*

## Parents' Top Ten Tax Tips List

1. Before you hire an experienced tax advisor, get references and consider what type of professional will work best with you and your family given your son's or daughter's talent and intended profession.

2. Once hired, listen carefully to the advice given.

3. Tax withholding calculated on Internal Revenue Service (IRS) Form W-4 should be completed and filed with each employer. A withholding calculator on the IRS website (www.irs.gov/Individuals/IRS-Withholding-Calculator) may assist you, alongside your tax advisor, to determine how many withholding allowances to claim and estimate tax. If your child will be subject to self-employment or other taxes, the

IRS website advises that you follow the instructions in Publication 505 to determine accurate withholding amounts. The more accurate the withholding, the less likely your child will owe taxes when tax season arrives.

4. Do not assume that taxes already paid during a given year are the only taxes that will be owed. This means that even though taxes may be withheld from a paycheck, additional taxes may be owed. Plan for this by setting aside money.

5. Keep records of all earnings inclusive of residuals. Software programs exist to make that easier for you to do. All tax documents should be placed in a separate folder, as soon as they arrive so that they can be easily furnished to the tax preparer. *Translation: Get it off the kitchen table!*

6. Keep contemporaneous records of everything you spend from your child's earnings and keep verifiable and legible receipts (yes, the hard copy paper kind). A contemporaneous record is one that is made or received in real time (and not three years later). In the event of a tax or court audit, those records and corresponding receipts may come in stupendously handy. With the advent of smartphones and the like, apps may be a real time-saver by assisting you with organization.

David K. Rogers, president of ActorsTaxPrep, Inc., a Los Angeles–based firm specializing in entertainment taxation, offers his perspective from his experience rooted in Southern California:

> There are over a hundred thousand people in the LA area filing tax returns listing themselves as an actor, and many more in other aspects of the entertainment industry. Accordingly, all but the newest auditors here are reasonably familiar with allowable performing arts deductions. This is markedly not true when we handle audits and/or mail in audits being conducted in other parts of the country—and that is simply because the percentage of entertainment pros is so much less, and therefore the auditors are far less likely to have encountered such returns before.[190]

Peter Jason Riley agrees. As an experienced CPA from the East Coast, Riley says, "The artist who gets audited will always have some conversation helping the agent to understand their business in conjunction

---

190  Personal interview with David K. Rogers, March 11, 2014.

with justifying and proving the specific deductions."[191] He advises holding on to receipts for ordinary and necessary expenses and being prepared to show how and why the deduction is ordinary and necessary.[192]

7. Keep separate records for what you spend from your own resources. Remember that you maintain the obligation to support your son or daughter, as long as he or she has not been declared emancipated. Here is language taken directly from a Superior Court Order Approving Contract of Minor:[193]

> *Please be advised:* California Family Code Section 6752(e) provides that a custodial parent or guardian holds for the benefit of a minor all of the minor's earnings under an entertainment- or sports-related contract. The parent or guardian must use such earnings to pay all liabilities incurred by the minor under the contract, including, but not limited to, payments for taxes on all earnings, including taxes on the amounts set aside, and

---

191 Peter Jason Riley, *New Tax Guide for Writers, Artists, Performers and Other Creative People.* Newburyport, MA: Focus Publishing/ R. Pullins Company, Inc., 2012, p. 139.

192 Ibid., p. 140.

193 Cal. Fam. Code, §6751.

payments for personal or professional services rendered to the minor or the business related to the contract. (Since the law requires that 15 percent of the minor's gross earnings be set aside in a blocked account, these obligations must be paid out of the remaining 85 percent payable under the contract.) Section 6752(e) also provides that nothing therein alters the parent or guardian's existing responsibilities to provide for the support of the minor child.

8. Pay taxes on a quarterly basis if and as advised by your tax preparer.

9. Keep a set of tax folders for your tax preparer. One folder should include tax documents (e.g., W-2 and 1099 statements reflective of income earned). Don't forget passive income, such as interest earned on investments, and so on. A second folder should contain a list of expenses incurred. Please make copies of what you provide to the tax preparer. Sometimes mistakes occur.

10. The money map that parents create should reflect all income earned against all expenses paid from income and earnings. That map should go to your son or daughter when you feel that the time is right. It

may be extremely helpful, if not downright valuable, to keep a log of what was going on with your child at the time, in terms of both work and career, in addition to what headwinds swirled inside the family. That way, your child is better able to place into perspective their income and earnings spent and saved against the expenses paid. For example, "That music producer didn't come cheap and you needed him so you could fulfill your contractual responsibilities at the time, which was when Dad had his appendicitis attack and Grandpa came to live with us." Not doing this but instead simply handing your son or daughter copies of aging tax returns won't tell the story. Placing yourself in your child's shoes, how satisfying would receipt of those returns be? Tax returns don't tell the personal story. (See Chapter 14, "Tables and Resources" for additional tax information.)

# CHAPTER 12

*Emancipation:*
*A Legal Escape Hatch for Kids*

Free at last! Free at last! Thank God
Almighty, we are free at last!

—Martin Luther King, Jr.[194]

Fictional star Joey becomes aware of bank withdrawal
slips that have no association with him or his career. He
thinks they came from his account because he knows the bank
and that the last four digits of the account number are 0878.
A Department of the Treasury notice has come directly to his
home for unpaid taxes owed by him, together with interest
and penalties churning away like a taxi meter. He overhears
neighbors telling his mom that she looks better than ever. She
shouts back by giving them the name of her "plastics guy." Joey's
younger brother has newly minted braces and is now going to
private school. The family just got a pretty nice car, too. Gone

194 Ending his "I Have a Dream" speech during the March on
Washington, August 28, 1967; from the Negro spiritual by
J. W. Work, "American Negro Songs" www.negrospirituals.com/
songs/free_at_last_from.htm.

is the Sunday morning ritual of clipping manufacturer coupons from the Sunday paper at the kitchen table. All these changes in family spending and saving occur after Joey's big break in television.

Joey's sinking realization that his paychecks may be his family's proverbial meal ticket makes him feel sick to his stomach. Understandably, feelings of fear, betrayal, anger, and isolation creep into his consciousness.

Reliance on his mother and her contributions complicate matters. Because Joey can't drive himself to work, he can't do what he is doing without his mother or, at the very least, the support of other grown-ups. His mother may be able to hire an on-set guardian or other similar person in her place since the television sitcom where Joey plays himself debuted as a mid-season replacement.

Joey represses his feelings, dogged by a demanding work schedule. Eventually, though, Uncle Sam and his state tax department catch up with Joey and the family. Pressure mounts in Joey's home. Everyone appears on edge. Joey heard about tax season when he was younger, but he couldn't ever figure out what that really meant, and he never had to pay taxes until now. He thinks his parents must know about tax season, and it confuses him that they hadn't planned to pay the taxes due by setting aside from his paychecks the money needed to pay them. After all, his money goes to them.

Let's add another dimension. The TV sitcom in which Joey acts features a traditional family, with Mom and Dad working outside the home to support the budding music career of Joey's character. As Joey memorizes his lines, script after script, he longs to have the simplicity of his television world in his personal and private life.

One Sunday morning, after the last batch of tax notices is received, Joey's mother wakes him up. She sits by the foot of his bed and says that he will have to work more to pay the taxes. He thinks to himself, "You spent the money. You should be paying for this." But he keeps quiet because he knows that driving with his mother to the studio will feel like an eternity if she is upset the whole time. Then when they get to the studio, she will start talking with the other moms behind his back. Forget it.

If you stop to consider Joey's experience, the resounding lament includes feelings of loss for childhood (especially when the child begins working at a very young age) and betrayal. Could anyone criticize a kid like Joey for craving some normalcy and for wanting his parents—who have either bungled his money or taken on management-type roles—to just be responsible parents?

## Legal Escape Hatch

The solution for a young performer in a situation such as Joey's could be a process called *emancipation*. The goal for the Joeys of the world is to stop the hemorrhaging of money and seize control of their career reins by being set free legally. How easy or hard it will be for a young performer to be "free" and what the legal world recognizes as an emancipated minor depend on state law and how he or she goes about getting it. States proceed cautiously with these requests, recognizing the special authority of parents to raise their kids as they deem fit, making decisions that are in their children's best interest along the way. According to the Supreme Court of the United States, "three reasons justifying the conclusion that the constitutional rights of children cannot be equated with those of adults [are] the peculiar vulnerability of children; their inability to make critical decisions in an informed, and mature manner; and the importance of the guiding role of parents in child rearing."[195]

*Note:* Due process rights are guaranteed in the US Constitution and are also defined in state constitutions: "No person shall . . . be deprived of life, liberty, or property, without due process of law." In particular, procedural due process

........................................................................

195  See *Bellotti v. Baird*, 443 US 622, 634 (1979).

entitles a person to notice and an opportunity to be heard before courts rule on a citizen's life, liberty, or property interest. Since children belong with their parents, any attempt to upset the status quo requires that the parents receive notice of the pleading filed and a court hearing.

Keeping it simple, the state in which a child resides determines how easy or difficult it will be for him or her to be set legally free. So if a child resides, for instance, in Redondo Beach, California, California law applies. And if a child resides in Nashville, Tennessee, Tennessee law applies.

In California, kids must prove to a court their current financial independence, which can be downright tricky to do. After all, a child's finances are generally inextricably entwined with the bills of the family household. That is the point for those kids who want out because they feel enslaved. If we think about the "best interest of the child" standard routinely used by state family courts to assess fair contracts and shared custody arrangements between parents and parental support obligations to meet a child's basic needs, then let's consider if a child's best interest is served when a child must show that he or she is managing his or her own financial affairs and living independently from his or her parent(s). In fact, over the years "a parallel has been made between California's emancipation statutes requiring minors (to) demonstrate financial independence and the Louisiana statutes for slave emancipation statutes which required that the slave demonstrate his ability to support himself upon emancipation."[196] The objective of both is to ensure that (the child or person) "will not become a burden to the society and . . . [sic] the minors will maintain sober habits and always be respectful."[197]

In plain English, legal goals ensure that kids, once emancipated, won't turn either to California taxpayers or to crime for support. Under the circumstances of the present day when a child's earnings are used to buy the house and pay the monthly mortgage payments, yet the deed to the house is titled in Mom's or Dad's name, is the child's best interest served or end-run by a conflicting law that says the child must prove that he or she managed his or her own affairs and lived independently? Over the years, people have leveled criticism at California for its unyielding and inconsistent standards on the issue. What do you think?

Setting aside these challenges, some California kids have managed to become emancipated, so it is possible. If and when

---

196 Davis, "A Matter of Trust," p. 76, citing Matthew Bennett, "Methods of Emancipation: Today's Children, Yesterday's Slaves," *Journal of Contemporary Legal Issues* 11 (1997): 632–634.

197 Bennett, "Methods of Emancipation," pp. 633–634, citing Judith Kelleher Schafer, "The Romanist Tradition in Louisiana: Legislation, Jurisprudence, and Doctrine: A Symposium," *Louisiana Law Review* 56 (1955): 409, 419.

a parent or parents eventually agree to the emancipation, the legal process becomes easier and the burden on the child to show actual proof to the court recedes, which is like turning a 26.2-mile marathon into a 5-mile run. When emancipation occurs, parents are no longer legally required to support their kids. In the context of young freedom fighters who seek a permanent vacation from supporting their parents (and possibly other family members, too), the law no longer legally requires that their parents support them. Well, that's a relief.

Lawyers who see repeated mismanagement of a child's funds lament that too few kids sue their parents. Placing the lawyers' lament into perspective, those circumstances comprise cases that, for the lawyer, open and close, are filed, then get stored and eventually purged or, at the client's election, picked up and toted home. Then, of course, the lawyers get to go home to their families. For talented working kids, in comparison, the path taken, the relationships that continue to evolve or end, and the emotional roller coaster and consequential scarring can last a lifetime.

Beyond the finances, the real world of 24-7, twenty-first century tabloid news can regrettably report a young performer seeking emancipation as a child divorcing his or her parents—as if kids didn't have enough emotional muck to wade through. Then, of course, the aftermath of emancipation can be downright isolating and terribly lonely for the young performer.

After all of this, what are the rights of an emancipated minor? An emancipated minor may likely count on the following:

- Being able to withdraw money from a bank or trust account(s) held for him or her
- Receiving every penny earned on a go-forward basis (except for fees spoken for by previously contracted agents, managers, or others)
- Choosing where to live

Other rights vary by state, so you cannot assume that every state gives emancipated minors the same rights, or if courts without a state emancipation law will even rule on the issue. Some *may* include the right to do the following:

- Sign contracts of all types, including for the purchase of real estate
- File, arbitrate, mediate, and ultimately settle lawsuits or bring them to trial
- Establish trusts for themselves and others
- Consent to medical treatment

*Cautionary note:* Emancipation does not guarantee exemption from child labor laws and regulations that are typically tied to age or school attendance laws in all fifty states, so check your state laws or regulations before taking action.

## Practical Advice for the Joeys of the World

If you are a young performer making plans to become emancipated, here's the quick and dirty. Emancipation is rare, so folks who staff other state offices may not even understand it. All they will see is that your birthday makes you fourteen years old and therefore a minor in their view. Whatever you do, do not leave the courthouse or the state without obtaining at least a few certified copies of the judgment, order, and/or ruling (state courts vary on what is issued). Don't be stingy about forking over money for these fancy copies because you will need them. Certified copies prove that the document is real and usually come embossed with a fancy or shiny seal. Then be patient as you find your way. If you find the going tough, there is no shame in leaning on former performers who have followed the same path or reaching out to a charity or foundation the mission of which includes helping young performers like you. Keep close one or two trusted friends who care about you and not about what your celebrity or fame can do for them. Finally, you may want to take action immediately, in which case enlisting the help of a lawyer may make a lot of sense. If there is a trusted relative in your family who happens to be a lawyer or paralegal, reach out first to him or her for help, for support. Whatever you choose to do, the public's recognition of your emancipation may require a lot of patience from you. After all, it's uncommon. Think of your emancipation as more of a process that may include educating others about your new legal status as opposed to being a red carpet destination.

*Final note:* If you are a working minor and what you have just read depresses you because you fear proving your case will not be possible, you may wish to consider learning more about guardianship and conservatorship. To put that in motion, a trusted family member or friend would petition the court to serve as your guardian and/or conservator (depending on the laws of your state and what you seek to accomplish).

# CHAPTER 13

*Website Support*

M any websites are dedicated to helping parents of talented kids. Without implying any endorsement, here are some that might get you started.

## For Former and Current Child Performers

*www.minorcon.org*

"Our mission is dedicated to helping young performers protect the earnings they generate," says founder Paul Petersen. He emphasizes education's great value in the lives of young performers. His organization continues to offer unwavering support and discretion to former and current working performers who need assistance.

*www.onlocationeducation.com*

Founded by Alan Simon, On Location Education is about education, on-location teachers (studio teachers and otherwise), and entertainment work permit processing for young performers.

*www.childreninfilm.com*

Founded by Toni Casala, Children in Film provides the "tools and information needed" to employ a child in the entertainment industry with entertainment work permit processing for young performers. Membership is available for online access to state work permit requirements.

*http://bizparentz.org*

Founded by Anne Henry and Paula Dorn, the BizParentz Foundation is a nonprofit company providing education, advocacy, and charitable support to parents and children in the entertainment industry.

*www.sagaftra.org/content/young-performers*

SAG-AFTRA works to attain fair pay, working conditions, and benefits for young performers.

*www.sagaftra.org/production-center*

SAG-AFTRA provides a variety of documents, from contracts to rate sheets.

*www.actorsequity.org*

The Actors' Equity Association is a labor union representing more than 50,000 members involved in live theatre productions.

# CHAPTER 14

*Tables and Resources*

*Advisory:* These resources are intended to assist you. However, they may or may not recite the actual law or all of the law on the subject. Moreover, the laws cited here do not generally include state work permitting requirements or regulations. (See Chapter 13, "Website Support" for work permitting resources.) The US Department of Labor compiles information by state, primarily of work permitting requirements and *select* state performance laws. Consequently, be advised that there is no replacement for the legal advice of an experienced attorney and connections to other professionals who can provide you with advice and service.

# *Tables*

This chapter contains the following helpful tables:

A.  States with Coogan-Type Laws and Other State Child Performer Laws (Contract Type)

B.  Education

C.  SAG-AFTRA Requirements for Adherence to Local Laws

D.  SAG-AFTRA Requirements for Medical Care and Safety/Dressing Rooms/Play Area

E.  Actors' Equity Association

## A. States with Coogan-Type Laws and Other State Child Performer Laws (Contract Type)

# States with Coogan-Type Laws

States with a Coogan-type law *require* that 15 percent of a child's gross earnings be placed into a particular account. New York, North Carolina, and Pennsylvania offer flexibility, by law, to seek more. The child generally receives his or her money on or after his or her eighteenth birthday, except in the earlier event of a trust bust or emancipation. To give you a sense of legislative activity by state, I provide dates of enactment and/ or recent amendment,[198] if any. Be careful here. Laws continue to evolve and change. Consequently, by the time you read this, other or continuing laws and amendments may have already been enacted, triggering new law or a change of law that is not reflected here.

---

198  The amendment date can vary from the date the law takes effect.

| State | Bank Account Type | Enactment or Amendment |
|-------|-------------------|------------------------|
| California[199] | Blocked-CA bank/brokerage Coogan Trust Account (CA Coogan type) | 1999, 2003, 2013[200] |
| New York[201] | u/t/m/a, u/g/m/a or Blocked-CA Coogan type | 2003, 2013 |
| Louisiana[202] | Blocked trust[203] | 2005, 2006[204] |
| New Mexico[205] | Trust where child resides | 2007[206] |
| North Carolina[207] | In trust[208] | 2003 |
| Pennsylvania[209] | Trust[210] or qualified tuition program | 2012 |

........................................................

199   Cal. Fam. Code §§6750–6753.

200   Exempts employer of minor under contractual services as an extra, background performer, or in a similar capacity to set aside 15 percent. See States with Child Performer Laws chart, below.

201   NY CLS EPTL §7-7.1 NY Child Performer Education and Trust Act of 2003. This is a mandatory requirement. See also NY CLS Labor §150 et seq. The elective court approval process is referenced as a child performer law. See States with Child Performer Laws chart, below.

202   La. R.S. §§51:2131–2133 applicable to any contract in which a minor is employed or agrees to render artistic or creative services for compensation of $500.00 or more.

203   Must be located in Louisiana unless trust account previously established on the minor's behalf in another state.

204   La. R.S. §51:2133. See States with Child Performer Laws chart, below.

205   N.M. Stat. Ann. §50-6-18–§50-6-19. See States with Child Performer Laws chart, below.

206   Fifteen percent of gross earnings for contracts of equal or greater than $1,000 US dollars or more not to be distributed until minor's eighteenth birthday, legal emancipation, or by court order.

207   N.C. Gen. Stat. §48A-11–§48A-18. See States with Child Performer Laws chart, below.

208   See States with Child Performer Laws chart, below.

209   43 P.S. §40.5. See States with Child Performer Laws chart, below.

210   Irrevocable.

*Pennsylvania Note:* As described above, Pennsylvania's law *requires* at least 15 percent of a minor's total compensation (before taxes, deductions, and commissions) to be deposited into either an irrevocable child performer trust account or a qualified tuition program if:

- the minor is entitled to receive residuals tied to a principal agreement; or
- earnings are anticipated to exceed $2,500; or
- the minor has already earned in excess of $2,500 in prior employment in performance.

A child performer trust account established in another state may be used.

## *Account Types*

State laws determine what type of account must be used to hold the money. The term *trust account* may reference different account types depending on state law. The following are general descriptions of some account types:

- A *blocked account* is specialized and locks in the money until the child turns eighteen, generally.
- A *u/t/m/a account* is an account established by the Uniform Trust to Minors Act or the Uniform Transfers to Minors Act.

- A *u/g/m/a account* is an account established by the Uniform Gifts to Minors Act.[211]

*Note to parents:* Shop around for financial institutions that offer the best interest rates and low maintenance fees, if any. An appeals court in California recently ruled that a bank, without court approval, could not charge and debit monthly service fees against Coogan trust accounts.[212]

## States with Child Performer Laws

States with child performer laws include California, New York, Louisiana, New Mexico, North Carolina, and Pennsylvania. These laws *may* include requirements for contract approval by a court and/or a designated set-aside of the child's earnings into an account other than a blocked or other designated account. Unless otherwise noted, the contract approval process is elective, not required. So, for example, New York has a mandatory 15 percent set-aside requirement *and* an elective court contract approval process.

---

211  Unless you live in a state where a court actively requires a trustee's duty to account to a court that will hopefully encourage protection from sticky fingers, u/t/m/a and u/g/m/a accounts can be easily raided because they are not sealed or routinely monitored. When the money is spent, it is gone.

212  *Phillips v. Bank of America, N.A.*, 2015 Cal. App. LEXIS 347.

| State | Court Contract Approval Process Available | Set-Aside | Dates of Enactment or Amendment |
|-------|------------------------------------------|-----------|--------------------------------|
| California | Yes | 15% | 1999, 2003, 2013[213] |
| Florida | Yes | Yes—Court sets amount[214] | 1995, 1997 |
| Illinois | Yes | No | 1990[215] |
| Kansas | Yes | 15%+[216] | 2000 |
| Louisiana | No | 15% | 2005, 2006[217] |
| Massachusetts | Yes[218] | Yes—Court sets amount | 1991, 1996 |
| Missouri | No | No | 1995[219] |
| Nevada | Yes | 15%–50%—Court sets amount[220] | 2003 |
| New Jersey | No | No | 1962, 1981[221] |
| New Mexico | No | 15%[222] | 2007 |
| New York | Yes | Court sets amount[223] | 1983, 1997, 2003, 2013[224] |
| North Carolina | Yes | 15%+[225] | 2003 |
| Pennsylvania | No | 15%+[226] | 2012 |
| Tennessee | Yes | 15%+[227] | 2003 |

..........................................................

213  Cal. Fam. Code §§6750–6753. Years do not apply to all sections.

214  Fla. Stat. §§743.08–743.095. If the child has no dependents, the court does not require a set-aside in excess of two-thirds of the minor's net earnings.

215  §§820 ILCS 20/0.01–20/2.

216  K.S.A. §§38-615–38-621. Mandatory set-aside, whether or not court approval of a contract is sought, applies to gross earnings equal to or greater than $5,000.00. Contract earnings and accumulations belong to the child. Child's parent, guardian, or guardian ad litem may request court to increase set-aside percentage at any time.

*Note to parents:* These and other laws and regulations are highly nuanced. What is presented here is only an excerpt. Consulting with a specialized attorney who can render advice

........................................................................

217 La. R.S. §§51:2131–2133 effective in 2005. La. R.S. 51:2133 amended in 2006. Mandatory set-aside of gross earnings.

218 ALM G.L. 231 §85p1/2. Mandatory court approval process excludes specified participating children.

219 §294.022 R.S.Mo. Safety is underscored, requiring a parent, guardian, or designated guardian to be present at all times at the place of a child's employment.

220 Net earnings: Nev. Rev. Stat. Ann. §609.470–§609.652. Elective process triggers the set-aside.

221 N.J. Stat. §34:2-21.58 et seq. (Employment of children under sixteen in theatrical productions.)

222 N.M. Stat. Ann. §50-6-18–§50-6-19. Trust account established in the state where minor resides for contracts equal or greater than $1,000.

223 Unless minor is entitled to his own earnings and has no dependents, court shall not require a set-aside of more than half of net earnings.

224 NY CLS Art & Cult Affr §35.01 enacted in 1983, amended in 2003 and 2013, NY CLS Art & Cult Affr §35.03 enacted in 1983, amended in 1997 and 2013.

225 N.C. Gen. Stat. §48A-11–§48A-18. Fifteen percent set-aside mandatory, with or without court approval of contract. The court may require more than 15 percent if requested by parent, guardian or minor through a guardian ad litem. Trust may be established in the United States or outside the United States.

226 43 P.S. §40.5. See Pennsylvania Note, above. (Total compensation prior to all taxes, deductions, and commissions.) At least 15 percent.

227 Tenn. Code Ann. §50-5-201–§50-5-222. The set-aside is 15 percent. The court may require more than 15 percent if requested by parent, guardian, or minor through guardian ad litem. Elective court process triggers the set-aside.

based on your circumstances as applied to the complete law of your state would be prudent.

## What Is a Trustee or Written Statement?

Although it varies by state, this document serves to identify the actual bank account and corresponding identifying information so that employers can make the deposit. Employers in California and New Mexico must provide a written acknowledgment that they received the written statement (e.g., a receipt).

*Note to parents:* Even if the controlling state law does not require an employer to issue a written statement, it would be a good idea for you to request one.

## What Is a Guardian Ad Litem?

Generally, a guardian ad litem, is a person designated by a state court to advance the interests of a child. The role varies by state. For states that follow the California model, a custodial parent may typically serve in this capacity. However, in the circumstance of a parent holding an ownership interest in a company contracting with their child, a court may then deem a conflict of interest exists, rendering the parent unsuitable to serve.

In other states, such as Massachusetts, the court would appoint a truly independent person to serve as a child's guardian ad litem, a person with no connection to the child or company if and when a guardian ad litem appointment is made. Comparatively, New York courts may appoint an independent person designated as a special guardian. The objective—in either of these situations and for other states that follow this protocol—is for the court to appoint a person who shares no interest in the child's money and contract but who stands tall and wise in the child's shoes.

## B. Education

### Parent and Production Company Resources

#### California Law

The following is taken directly from the legal text. This is an excerpt only. See the law for all information.

1.  Employers shall provide a studio teacher on each call for minors from age fifteen (15) days to their sixteenth (16th) birthday (age sixteen, 16), and for minors from age sixteen (16) to age eighteen (18) when required for the education of the minor. One (1) studio teacher

must be provided for each group of ten (10) minors or fraction thereof. With respect to minors age fifteen (15) days to age sixteen (16), one studio teacher must be provided for each group of twenty (20) minors or fraction thereof on Saturdays, Sundays, holidays, or during school vacation periods.[228]

2. When minors resident in the State of California and employed by an employer in the entertainment industry located in . . . California, are taken from the State of California to work on location in another state, as part of, and pursuant to, contractual arrangements made in the State of California for their employment in the entertainment industry, the child labor laws and the regulations based thereon shall be applicable, including, but not limited to, the requirement that a studio teacher must be provided for such minor . . .[229] (Alaska requires day-one instruction by a studio teacher.)

3. SAG-AFTRA, pursuant to its 2005 Theatrical Agreement,[230] recognizes that when minors are employed in the State of California or taken from the State of California pursuant to a contract made

---

228  Cal. Code Regs. tit. 8, § 11755.2.

229  Cal. Code Regs. tit. 8, § 11756.

230  Section 50 "Employment of Minors."

in California, California laws and regulations follow them.

## Other Resources

- See the "California Child Labor Laws" publication available at www.dir.ca.gov/DLSE/ChildLaborLawPamphlet.pdf.
- *Blue Book: Employment of Minors in the Entertainment Industry*, Studio Teachers, IATSE, Local 884. Standards and practices for the hiring and employment of underage performers in the film and television industries.

## New York Law[231]

The following is taken directly from the legal text. This is an excerpt only. See the law for all information.

1. Satisfactory academic performance is required to obtain or renew a work permit.

2. The child performer's school district determines the criteria of satisfactory performance.

......................................................................

231  NY CLS Labor §154-a, Subpart 186-5.1; and "Child Performer Education Requirements: Frequently Asked Questions," www.labor.state.ny.us/workerprotection/laborstandards/secure/child/cp_academics2.shtm#2.

3. No child performer required by law to be enrolled and attend school can be without educational instruction and unemployed for more than ten consecutive days while school is in session.

4. School officials have the authority to develop alternative methods a performer may use to satisfy educational requirements. A child performer receiving instruction from an employer-provided teacher must not be declared absent from school while working.

5. Employers are required to provide (this means pay for) a teacher[232] for a child performer when:

    a. School is in session; and

        i. From the 3rd day of missed instruction through the remainder of the child's employment in the production; or

    b. From the 1st day of missed instruction through the remainder of the child's employment if the child was guaranteed 3 or more consecutive days of employment.

......................................................................

232 This means a teacher who is certified or has credentials recognized by New York State.

*Other Resources*

- See New York State Department of Labor "Child Performer Frequently Asked Questions," at www.labor.ny.gov/workerprotection/laborstandards/secure/Child PerformerFAQ.shtm.

- See New York State Department of Education, Office of Teaching Initiatives at www.highered.nysed.gov/tcert/home.html and www.highered.nysed.gov/tcert/certificate/teachrecother.html regarding Interstate Reciprocity to receive an Initial certificate to teach in New York.

## C. SAG-AFTRA Requirements for Adherence to Local Law[233]

1.  SAG-AFTRA, pursuant to Section 50 (Employment of Minors) in its Basic Agreement, says that *any* contract provision that is inconsistent and less restrictive than the child labor law or regulation in the applicable state or jurisdiction where the minor is working shall be modified to comply with that law or regulation. This also means that the terms of the union agreement shall

---

233  SAG-AFTRA approved.

prevail over inconsistent or less restrictive terms, including those states or jurisdictions where there are no laws or regulations in place where the minor is working. *Example:* If a minor is working in a state without a sight and/or sound requirement, the union's sight and sound requirement controls, whether or not the minor is a California resident.

2. Be mindful that the Producer's requirement to determine and comply with a prevailing local law is applicable when the Producer is SAG-AFTRA affiliated. For nonunion productions, the outcome varies depending upon the production company's policies and protocol. Local compliance, however, is the prudent way to go.

To see the complete agreement that includes Section 50 (Employment of Minors), go to www.sagaftra.org/files/sag/2005TheatricalAgreement.pdf.

## D. SAG-AFTRA Requirements for Medical Care and Safety/Dressing Rooms/Play Area[234]

1. The minor's parent or guardian must provide Producer a certificate signed by a doctor licensed to practice

......................................................................

234 Reprinted with permission by SAG-AFTRA.

medicine within the state wherein the minor resides or is employed, stating that the minor has been examined within six (6) months prior to the date he or she was engaged by Producer and has been found to be physically fit.

2. Prior to a minor's first call, Producer must obtain the written consent of the minor's parent or legal guardian for medical care in the case of an emergency. However, if the parent or legal guardian refuses to provide such consent because of religious convictions, Producer must at least obtain written consent for external emergency aid, provided that the obtaining of such consent is not contrary to the aforementioned religious convictions.

3. No minor shall be required to work in a situation which places the child in clear and present danger to life or limb. If a minor believes he/she would be in such danger, the parent or guardian may have the teacher and/or stunt coordinator, if either or both are present, discuss the situation with the minor. If the minor persists in his/her belief, regardless of its validity, the minor shall not be required to perform in such situation.

4. When a minor is asked to perform physical, athletic, or acrobatic activity of an extraordinary nature, the

minor's parent or guardian shall first be advised of the activity and shall represent that the minor is fully capable of performing the activity. Producer will comply with reasonable requests for equipment that may be needed for safety reasons.

## Dressing Rooms

No dressing rooms shall be occupied simultaneously by a minor and an adult performer or by minors of the opposite sex.

## Play Areas

A safe and secure place for minors to rest and play must be provided by Producer.

## E.　　Actors' Equity Association

Equity's rules are not the same as those for SAG-AFTRA. Moreover, rules vary per agreement and therefore are not uniform. Consequently, you must carefully review the agreement to know the terms under which your child is working. However, I am including an excerpt of the following Equity/League

Production Contract to offer you guidelines in that contractual circumstance in order to offer you contrast.

## Equity/League Production Contract[235]

35. *Juvenile Actors (excerpt only)*

A. The following special provisions shall apply to all Actors who are *both* under 19 years of age at the time of signing and who have not completed high school:

1. Juvenile Actor may not be called to understudy or brush-up rehearsals which would intrude on the Actor's normal school day more than once per calendar week.

2. Producer shall be responsible for providing services of an accredited or licensed tutor while the company is on tour and during period of out-of-town tryout or previews at Point of Organization during the Actor's applicable school year until one week following the Official Opening at the

---

235 Actors' Equity Association, *Agreement and Rules Governing Employment Under the Equity/League Production Contract*, www.actorsequity.org/docs/rulebooks/Production_Rulebook_League_11-15.pdf, effective date: September 26, 2011, expiration date: September 27, 2015. Reprinted with permission from Actors' Equity Association.

Point of Organization. Tutors shall be required to familiarize themselves with the reasonable and customary schooling requirements of the Juvenile Actors by the first day of rehearsal.

3. During the rehearsal period, prior to Official Opening at Point of Organization or first paid public performance on tour, up to six hours per week of required tutoring must be held during the permitted rehearsal hours. However, when the Juvenile Actors are rehearsing and/or performing on "10 out of 12" hour days, all required tutoring must be held during the permitted rehearsal hours.

4. If rehearsals for a Juvenile replacement Actor intrude on the Actor's normal school hours for more than 10 school days prior to Actor's first paid public performance or Official Opening, whichever is later, then an accredited or licensed tutor shall be offered.

5. For Juvenile Actors between 16 and 18 years of age, Producer shall use best efforts to schedule publicity assignments in accordance with Rule 52 PHOTOGRAPHS, PUBLICITY AND PROMOTION, so as not to interfere with Actor's normal school

day. For Juvenile Actors under 16 years of age, see (B)(2) below.

6. *Working Papers.* To the extent working papers may be required by law, a copy of the Juvenile's working papers must be filed with Equity by the Juvenile's first day of rehearsal.

B. The following special provisions shall apply to Actors under 16 years of age at the time of signing.

1. Producer shall provide a responsible person to supervise Juvenile Actors during the rehearsal period and, after the first public performance, from half-hour until Juvenile Actor is called for by a responsible parent or guardian after curtain down. Such person shall not be assigned any other duty under jurisdiction of Equity or another theatrical craft Union which conflicts with the supervision of Juvenile Actors.

2. Juvenile Actors under 16 years of age shall be permitted to accept publicity assignments in accordance with Rule 52, PHOTOGRAPHS, PUBLICITY AND PROMOTION, provided such activities do not interfere with the Actor's normal school day.

3. A Juvenile Actor may be signed to a Six-Month Term Contract in accordance with Rule 16(H)(1), CONTRACTS.

4. Whenever Juvenile Actor is required to live away from Actor's permanent residence as registered with Equity and further provided the Juvenile Actor is traveling with a parent or legal guardian not regularly employed in the production, Producer, in addition to any other payments required, shall pay Juvenile Actor not less than one-third of minimum Per Diem required by Rule 63(B), or Rule 70(B)(2)(c) for Tiered Tours.

5. *Dressing Rooms.* If available, separate dressing rooms for male and female Juveniles will be provided and shall be separate from the adult dressing rooms.

34. *Intimidation (applies to all actors)*

A. An Actor shall not be compelled to participate in encounter groups, sensitivity sessions, or classes which Actor deems dangerous to Actor's mental health or an infringement upon Actor's mental or physical privacy.

B. If an Actor makes claim in writing to Equity within seven days that Actor was intimidated into terminating his contract by being compelled to participate in such encounter group, sensitivity session, or class, Equity shall promptly notify the Producer. If such intimidation is acknowledged or established, the Actor shall be reinstated and shall be made whole for any loss.

C. Neither the Producer, nor any personnel under the Producer's supervision or control, shall intentionally intimidate, harass, or humiliate any Actor at any time, including, but not limited to, all communications to Actors in connection with artistic notes. However, it is understood that there is no intent to interfere with the original Director's or original Choreographer's ability to critique Actors in connection with artistic notes.

37.   *Law Governing (excerpt only)*

A. All contracts of employment shall be subject to, be construed by and all the rights of the parties thereto shall be determined by the laws of the State of New York, except as otherwise may be provided.

B. If there are any valid provisions of law applicable to a contract of employment which are in conflict herewith, the provisions of the contract which conflict therewith shall be deemed modified in conformity with provisions of such applicable laws.

If you have questions, call an Equity Business Representative. See http://actorsequity.org for more information.

# ACKNOWLEDGMENTS

For all those who interviewed with me, on and "off record" and gave of their talents, time, and experience with particular recognition to Paul Petersen.

Also to Meghan Harvey at Girl Friday Productions. Former research assistants Kristen Fennell, JD, whose passion about child labor law and associated protections distinguished her research work, and Kevin R. Kahn, Esq., whose commitment and thoroughness made his research work notable.

God bless the folks at the California State Hall of Records in Los Angeles and especially one hardworking soul. After flying more than 2,500 miles to do legal research, I found myself way below street level in the bowels of the microfilm department, passing, along the way, a tattered poster that offered precautions in the event of an earthquake. An unassuming man named Nestor got me through. As I wove my way down a labyrinth of tired blue elevators, holes in windowless walls, stale air, and stairways that reflected the apparently starved state of government budgets, I realized pretty quickly that I was light-years away from the Kodak Theatre's red carpet and that I would need more than a few prayers to chisel case records from the 1930s. Any possible doubts I harbored about the working conditions in that building were dispelled as I read a handwritten sign taped to a water cooler that read, "If you are not in the Water Club, do not drink the water!" As I extended my hand in a small gesture of appreciation for showing me how to work really old machines and dutifully fetching multiple films that I had requested, Nestor confided that he was "new" and that he used to work across the street. I left that basement grateful that he was there to help me. Madeline Cueroni for her ongoing encouragement. The late Barry E. Rosenthal, Esq., for his assessment of my potential. His belief sustained my momentum in practice over the years and during the research and writing stages of this book. Most especially to Lou Gaglini. He knows why.

# ABOUT THE AUTHOR

Photo courtesy of Steve Robb

Sally R. Gaglini is the founder of the Gaglini Law Group LLC and an adjunct faculty member at Suffolk University Law School, where she teaches entertainment law. She has spent more than twenty-five years advising talented young artists and their families as well as companies working with young talent and promoting their artistry. Gaglini's specialized expertise began with her involvement with emerging boy bands as they established their music careers. She proposed and authored, with lawmakers, the inaugural child performer law in Massachusetts. Drawing on her deep industry knowledge that includes experience with families as a courtroom advocate, court-appointed fiduciary, and guardian ad litem, Gaglini's unique credentials blend the entertainment and advertising industries with family and probate law. The author is an AV-rated lawyer who was recently honored as one of the "Top Women of Law" in 2014 by *Massachusetts Lawyers Weekly*. For more information, please visit www.gaglinilaw.com and www.youngperformersatwork.com.

# INDEX

## E

## O